Freeze Drying Cookbook

The Essential guide to master the art of preserving food with easy & tasty Recipes and long-lasting storage techniques

David Hunt

Table of Contents

Introduction 7
A Brief Overview and Its History
Benefits of Freeze-Drying for Long-Term Preservation
Making the Most of Your Garden Harvests
The Advantage for Outdoor Activities
Lightweight and Nutritious

Chapter 1 9
Understanding Freeze-Drying
Types of Freeze-Drying
Stages of the Freeze-Drying Process
Expert Guidelines for Storing Freeze-Dried Food
Criteria for Identifying High-Quality Freeze-Dried Food
Effective Methods for Rehydrating Freeze-Dried Food

Chapter 2 11
Practical Applications of Freeze-Drying
Freeze-Drying Food: What Works and What Doesn't
Non-Food Applications of Freeze-Drying
Using Freeze-Drying to Preserve Harvests

Chapter 3 13
The Science Behind Freeze-Drying
Fundamental Principles
Heat and Mass Transfer in Freeze-Drying
The Role of Vacuum and Pressure in the Process
Effects of freeze-drying on Humans and animals' Health

Chapter 4 15
Freeze-Drying Equipment and Technology
Overview of Freeze-Drying Equipment:
Advancements in Freeze-Drying Technology:

Chapter 5 17
Troubleshooting and Maintenance
Common Issues in Freeze-Drying and How to Fix Them
Maintenance of Your Freeze-Drying Machine
Expanding and Improving Freeze-Drying Operations

Chapter 6 19
Quality Control in Freeze-Drying
Importance of Quality Control
Parameters to Monitor
Common Quality Issues and Solutions

Chapter 7 23
The Rehydration Process in Freeze-Dried Foods
The Basic Rehydration Process
Rehydration of Different Food Types
Factors Affecting the Rehydration Process

Breakfast.. 26
Freeze-Dried Berry and Yogurt Parfait
Overnight Oats with Freeze-Dried Fruits
Freeze-Dried Smoothie Bowl
Healthy Pancakes with Freeze-Dried Berries
Homemade Muesli with Freeze-Dried Fruits and Nuts
Protein-Packed Quinoa Porridge with Freeze-Dried Fruits
Avocado Toast with Freeze-Dried Tomatoes
Vegan Chia Pudding with Freeze-Dried Mango
Whole Grain Muffins with Freeze-Dried Blueberries
Egg Scramble with Freeze-Dried Veggies

Snacks.. 38
Freeze-Dried Tropical Fruit Salad
Crunchy Freeze-Dried Veggie Chips
Protein-Packed Greek Yogurt with Freeze-Dried Berries
Freeze-Dried Apple and Almond Butter Sandwiches
Spiced Chickpea Crunchies with Freeze-Dried Spinach
Peanut Butter Energy Balls with Freeze-Dried Raspberries
Freeze-Dried Edamame and Quinoa Salad
Sweet and Spicy Freeze-Dried Mango Salsa
Freeze-Dried Vegetable Hummus Dip
Spicy Roasted Chickpeas with Freeze-Dried Seasonings

Lunch.. 50
Freeze-Dried Vegetable Stir Fry with Tofu
Salmon Salad with Freeze-Dried Citrus Dressing
Spiced Chicken and Freeze-Dried Vegetable Soup
Beef Stroganoff with Freeze-Dried Mushrooms
Quinoa Salad with Freeze-Dried Beets and Avocado
Shrimp Paella with Freeze-Dried Peas and Bell Peppers
Turkey Chili with Freeze-Dried Corn and Tomatoes
Pork Stir Fry with Freeze-Dried Pineapple and Broccoli
Freeze-Dried Black Bean and Corn Burritos
Chicken Shawarma Wraps with Freeze-Dried Cucumbers
Chicken Alfredo with Sun-Dried Tomatoes and Spinach
Beef & Vegetable Skewers with Bell Peppers and Onions
Vegan Pad Thai with Freeze-Dried Tofu and Bean Sprouts
Seafood Gumbo with Freeze-Dried Okra and Shrimp
Turkey Meatballs with Freeze-Dried Cranberries and Sag
Lamb Tagine with Freeze-Dried Apricots and Chickpeas
Tofu and Bamboo Shoots Vegan Thai Green Curry
Crab Cakes with Freeze-Dried Corn and Red Bell Pepper
Caesar Salad with Freeze-Dried Romaine and Croutons
Lentil Soup with Freeze-Dried Carrots and Celery

Dinner 72
Freeze-Dried Vegetable Ratatouille with Grilled Chicken

Seafood Paella with Freeze-Dried Mussels and Shrimp
Roasted Pork Loin with Freeze-Dried Apricot and Sage
Beef Bourguignon with Freeze-Dried Pearl Onions and Mushrooms
Vegan Shepherd's Pie with Freeze-Dried Lentils and Root Vegetables
Spaghetti Marinara with Freeze-Dried Shrimp and Basil
Chicken Tagine with Freeze-Dried Apricots & Chickpeas
Grilled Steak with Freeze-Dried Chimichurri Sauce
Vegan Soba Noodle Soup with Freeze-Dried Tofu and Vegetables
Bouillabaisse with Freeze-Dried Seafood and Fennel
Roast Duck with Freeze-Dried Plum Sauce and Bok Choy
Lamb Curry with Freeze-Dried Peas and Potatoes
Vegan Stuffed Bell Peppers with Freeze-Dried Quinoa and Black Beans
Lobster Thermidor with Freeze-Dried Mushrooms
Chicken Marsala with Freeze-Dried Mushrooms
Beef and Broccoli Stir-Fry with Freeze-Dried Peppers and Sesame Seeds
Vegan Thai Green Curry with Freeze-Dried Bamboo Shoots and Eggplant
Seafood Linguine with Freeze-Dried Clams and Parsley
Chicken & Sausage Gumbo with Freeze-Dried Okra
Lentil and Vegetable Curry with Freeze-Dried Spinach and Cauliflower
Dessert..**94**
Freeze-Dried Strawberry and Banana Parfait
Chocolate Mousse with Freeze-Dried Raspberries
Vanilla and Freeze-Dried Berry Chia Pudding
Freeze-Dried Peach and Almond Tart
Freeze-Dried Mango and Coconut Sorbet
Ricotta Cheesecake with Freeze-Dried Blueberry
Chocolate Chip Cookies with Freeze-Dried Cherries
Vegan Chocolate Pudding with Freeze-Dried Raspberries
Freeze-Dried Apple and Cinnamon Crumble
Lemon and Freeze-Dried Blackberry Shortbread Bars
Conclusion...**107**
The Future of Freeze-Drying
Emerging Trends and Innovations
Appendix **108**

WE HAVE A GIFT FOR YOU!

Our special <u>Bonus</u> will enrich your reading experience. This book has many supplementary materials to enhance your comprehension, knowledge, skills, and information.

<u>YOU WILL FIND THE BONUS GIFT AT THE END OF THE BOOK!</u>

Introduction

Welcome to the complete guide to freeze-drying. This book is for anyone who wants to learn more about the background, benefits, and real-world uses of freeze-drying, whether they are home gardeners, adventurers, or just interested in preserving food.

Freeze-drying, also called lyophilization, is one of the best ways to keep food fresh and its quality and nutritional value. It lets you eat food from your garden all year long and gives you easy-to-make, light meals for outdoor activities.

This book talks about how freeze-drying works, from the different kinds to the steps of the process, as well as how to store and rehydrate things properly. It details the science behind freeze-drying and how it can be used to make food. Lastly, we'll discuss common problems and how to care for your freeze-drying machine.

A Brief Overview and Its History

Freeze-drying, called lyophilization in the science world, is a great way to store food because it keeps the structure and nutritional profile of the food very well. Through freezing and then vacuum-induced sublimation, the product's water content is effectively removed. This makes the product much lighter and very durable.

This method is interesting because it has a long history. Freeze-drying started with the ancient Incas of the Andes, who naturally used high altitude and cold weather to freeze-dry potatoes. During World War II, the process was improved so blood plasma could be kept for injuries on the battlefield without being held in a fridge. After the war, freeze-drying was used more in the food business, pharmaceuticals, and other places.

As we learn about freeze-drying, we will examine how it works and figure out the science behind it. We'll build a strong understanding of freeze-drying, which will help us move on to more practical, hands-on topics in the following chapters.

Benefits of Freeze-Drying for Long-Term Preservation

Freeze-drying is an excellent way to keep food for a long time, and it has many benefits that make it better than usual methods like canning or dehydrating. Freeze-drying keeps the quality, nutritional value, color, and taste of foods by carefully removing the water content while maintaining the food's structure. What makes freeze-drying special is how it affects the food's shelf life. Freeze-dried foods can be kept safely for years, even decades, without refrigeration. Even though these foods have been stored for a long time, they bring back their original flavor and nutritional value when rehydrated, making them taste as fresh as the day they were kept.

Making the Most of Your Garden Harvests

For people who like gardening, freeze-drying is an exciting and valuable way to maximize your garden harvests. Imagine a world where you could enjoy the taste of your home-grown fruits and veggies all year long, regardless of the seasons. Have you just picked a lot of tomatoes, berries, or other fruits and vegetables? Freeze-drying lets you catch these foods when they are at their best, so you can spend less and always have healthy, garden-fresh food on your table, regardless of the season.

The Advantage for Outdoor Activities

Lightweight and Nutritious

Freeze-dried foods are great for people whose hearts beat in time with nature. When going climbing, camping, backpacking, or doing anything else outside, freeze-dried foods are a huge help because they are small and light. These foods are not only easy to carry around, but they are also easy to make. All you need to do is add water for a tasty, nutritious meal. Freeze-dried meals can keep you going on day walks or longer trips into the backcountry without making your pack too heavy.

In this book, you'll not only learn about the science behind freeze-drying, but you'll also find out how to put this knowledge to use in the real world. This book gives you a complete toolkit for freeze-drying. It has a thorough guide to the freeze-drying process, helpful tips for storing and rehydrating freeze-dried foods, and a collection of delicious recipes for freeze-drying a wide range of meals, fruits, and vegetables.

Chapter 1
Understanding Freeze-Drying

Types of Freeze-Drying

When it comes to freeze-drying, there are two main ways to do it: the tray method and the various method.

• Tray-Style Freeze-Drying: This method uses a shelf tray system inside a freeze-drying chamber. It is often used in large-scale industrial processes. The lyophilization process takes place on these trays, where the material to be kept is spread out.

• Manifold Freeze-Drying: This method is different because the material is flash-frozen and put straight into the drying room. It is best for smaller-scale or home-based operations. The next step is the same as the one before. The material is put in a vacuum, which allows the frozen water to sublimate.

Freeze-drying and lyophilization are both terms that mean the same thing. The word "lyophilization" comes from the Greek words "lyo," which means "to set free," and "philos," which means "loving." It's a good name because the process takes advantage of the fact that, under certain conditions (low pressure and heat), water can skip the liquid phase and go straight from a solid (ice) to a gas (vapor).

This method has several benefits over other food storage methods, like canning and dehydrating. Freeze-drying doesn't need additives like canning, and because the process uses low heat, the food keeps its shape and structure. When compared to dehydrating, freeze-drying takes about 95% of the water content, much more than dehydrating.

Stages of the Freeze-Drying Process

The freeze-drying process comprises three essential steps for preparing the material for long-term keeping. The process is straightforward and follows a set order, which keeps the material in the best shape.

• The first step of freeze-drying is pre-freezing. The food or materials are spread out properly on trays and then in a freezer. This is usually done in a special freezer, ensuring the freezing process is even. For faster results, flash freezing can also be used. By freezing the material, its structure and makeup become more stable, which lets it keep its original shape as it dries. The size and shape of the ice crystals that form during pre-freezing can significantly affect the quality of the end product. This is because the temperature and speed at which pre-freezing is done affect the size and speed of pre-freezing. When you freeze something quickly, you get smaller crystals, which are usually better for the end product.

• Primary Drying (Sublimation): After the material has been pre-frozen, it is put in the freeze-drying room, and a vacuum is made. The room is heated slowly and carefully, which causes the ice inside the material to change directly from a solid to a gas. This is called sublimation. It's important to remember that this process skips the liquid phase, so the frozen water goes straight from solid to gas. This step can take up to 70% of the total drying time and is the longest part of the process.

• Secondary Drying (Desorption): Some linked water molecules remain in the material after sublimation. The goal of the second drying step is to get rid of this remaining moisture. While keeping the vacuum, the temperature is raised even more, which makes it easier for the leftover water molecules to leave the material. By reducing the liquid content to less than 1%, secondary drying ensures that the freeze-dried material will stay stable and good for a long time.

After these steps, the freeze-dried material is put in a package that can't let wetness in. This keeps the product from getting wet again from humidity in the air and keeps it for a long time.

Expert Guidelines for Storing Freeze-Dried Food

The key to keeping freeze-dried food fresh and lasting long is storing it correctly. It's crucial to put freeze-dried food in containers that keep out air and light since light can make food go bad over time. You can use metal cans, Mylar bags with oxygen filters, or mason jars sealed with a vacuum. Once the food is packed, it should be kept somewhere cool, dry, and dark. Heat, wetness, and light can all speed up the process of food going bad, shortening its shelf life and making it less tasty.

Criteria for Identifying High-Quality Freeze-Dried Food

There are a few things that show how good freeze-dried food is. First, the food should keep its original shape and color, even though the lack of water will make it look much drier and lighter. Second, good freeze-dried food should work well when rehydrated. It should return to its original texture and taste in a few minutes after adding water. If the food is still hard after soaking or smells or tastes bad, it could mean it was freeze-dried, stored wrong, or past its prime.

Effective Methods for Rehydrating Freeze-Dried Food

Rehydrating freeze-dried food is a process that is relatively uncomplicated and quick. A small amount of warm water, just enough to rehydrate the food without making it soggy, should be added to the dish. To rehydrate freeze-dried ingredients for soups, stews, or sauces, whisk them into the dish and cook them until the components are completely rehydrated. However, because different foods rehydrate at different rates, it is vital to check on them at regular intervals to prevent them from over-soaking. After being rehydrated, the food must be eaten.

Chapter 2
Practical Applications of Freeze-Drying

Freeze-drying is a very useful method that can be used for many things, from preserving food to making medicines. In this chapter, we'll look at how freeze-drying can be used in the real world, including food and non-food uses.

Freeze-Drying Food: What Works and What Doesn't

When it comes to storing food, freeze-drying is a game-changer. Almost any food, from fruits, vegetables, and meats to dairy items and complete meals, can be freeze-dried. But not all things can be freeze-dried in the same way.

- What Works Well: Many fruits and veggies freeze-dry beautifully, keeping their original shape, color, and texture once rehydrated. Some of these are berries, apples, peaches, carrots, peppers, and potatoes. Meat and poultry can also easily freeze-dried, especially when cooked and cut into small pieces. Also, ready-to-eat foods like pasta, rice dishes, soups, and stews can be freeze-dried to prepare meals and only need hot water.
- What doesn't work as well: It's hard to freeze dry foods with a lot of sugar or fat because sugar melts during the process, and fat doesn't dry. Because of this, freeze-dried foods like bacon or high-sugar fruits like figs can have a feel that isn't the best. Also, freeze-dried foods, mostly water, like watermelon or cucumber, often lose their original shape and become crumbly.

Non-Food Applications of Freeze-Drying

Freeze-drying is usually thought of as a way to keep food fresh, but it has other uses that are just as impressive:

- Pharmaceuticals: Freeze-drying is used in the pharmaceutical business to keep vaccines, antibiotics, and other biological materials stable and to make them last longer. It makes it possible to keep these fragile substances without making them less valuable.

- Preserving Flowers: Freeze-drying can also preserve flowers, keeping their shape and color for much longer than other drying methods. This method is often used to make keepsake flowers or to study plants.

- Recovering Important Paper Documents or Books: Freeze-drying is an excellent way to save and repair important paper documents or books damaged by water. It helps remove the moisture without bending the paper or making the ink run.

- Restoring pottery and other ceramics: Freeze-drying is also used in archaeology to save pottery and other ceramics ruined by water. It lets the water be taken out without hurting or changing the item.

This wide range of uses shows how flexible freeze-drying is as a way to keep things fresh. If you're interested in preserving food or want to look into its scientific benefits, knowing how freeze-drying works and what it can be used for can open up a world of possibilities.

Using Freeze-Drying to Preserve Harvests

You can't say enough about how important freeze-drying is for keeping crops. First of all, it is a powerful tool for fighting food waste, which is a big problem all over the world. Many fruits, veggies, and other grown crops go to waste every year because they aren't eaten in time. This waste is not only a waste of money but also worsens environmental problems like greenhouse gas pollution.

Freeze-drying is a long-term way to solve this situation. By freeze-drying extra food, farmers, gardeners, and customers can keep it at its most nutritious for months or even years without adding chemicals or putting it in the fridge.

Also, freeze-drying crops at their peak of ripeness look in nutrients that would otherwise be lost over time. This ensures that the food is as healthy as possible when eaten later. This can be helpful in places or times of the year when fresh fruits and veggies are hard to find.

On a larger scale, freeze-dried food's long shelf life and light weight mean that it doesn't need to be moved and stored as often, which saves energy and reduces our carbon footprint. So, freeze-drying fits in with global attempts to make the food system more sustainable and wasteful.

Chapter 3
The Science Behind Freeze-Drying

This part will explain the basic scientific ideas that explain how freeze-drying works. The goal is to give you a complete scientific understanding of freeze-drying, from the role of heat and mass transfer to the value of vacuum and pressure and the key idea of sublimation.

Fundamental Principles

Freeze-drying is based on some basic science ideas, with sublimation being the most important. Sublimation is when a material goes from a solid (like ice) to a gas (like vapor) without going through a liquid state. In the case of freeze-drying, this lets water be taken out of a product without changing its shape or nutritional value. To understand how freeze-drying works, you have to understand this concept.

Heat and Mass Transfer in Freeze-Drying

The process of freeze-drying requires careful handling of heat and mass transfer:

• Transfer of heat: When a product is freeze-dried, heat is slowly added to it. This heat is needed to speed up sublimation, which is the straight change of ice in the product into vapor. How long it takes to freeze-dry something depends significantly on how quickly heat passes. You must find the right mix to dry something quickly without damaging it.

• Mass transfer: Mass transfer is just as important to the freeze-drying process as heat transfer. As the ice in the product melts and turns into water vapor, this vapor needs to be constantly pulled out of the freeze-drying room to keep the vacuum there. Like the heat transfer rate, the mass transfer rate directly affects the time it takes to freeze-dry something.

The Role of Vacuum and Pressure in the Process

When something is freeze-dried, vacuum and pressure are very important. The process takes place in a low-pressure setting made possible by a vacuum. This low pressure makes it possible for the water in the food to sublimate at lower temperatures than it would if the stress was every day. Keeping the right amount of vacuum is a delicate balance. If the pressure is off, the product won't dry well or might get damaged.

Effects of freeze-drying on Humans and animals' Health

When it comes to the health benefits of freeze-dried foods, both people and pets can get a lot out of this way of food preservation. Since freeze-drying doesn't use high temps, most of the food's nutrients, such as vitamins and antioxidants, are kept. This means freeze-dried food is more like fresh food in terms of its nutritional value than other ways of preserving food, such as freezing or drying.

Freeze-dried food can be a healthy and easy way to feed your pet. It can give pets a meal similar to what they would eat in the wild, and the main ingredient is often real, high-quality meat. As with human food, most of the nutrients in freeze-dried pet food remain, giving dogs a balanced and healthy diet. However, talking to a vet about your pet's diet is always important to get specific advice.

Chapter 4
Freeze-Drying Equipment and Technology

The freeze-drying process is very careful and depends greatly on the tools and technology used. This part details the different kinds of freeze-drying equipment, their importance, and the latest innovations that make freeze-drying easier and faster.

Overview of Freeze-Drying Equipment:

Free-drying equipment covers a wide range, from large, complicated machines used in factories to small, easy-to-use machines used at home daily. No matter how big or small the gadget is, it has a few key parts needed for the freeze-drying process.

Every freeze-drying system has a room, a vacuum pump to lower the pressure, a condenser to collect the sublimated vapor, and a heating system to give the sublimation process the energy it needs. These parts work together in a carefully planned order to keep your goods safe.

Large industrial freeze-dryers might look scary, but we're lucky to live in a time when the technology has been shrunk into much smaller, easier-to-use units. With these home-use tools, artists, small business owners, and home gardeners can use this high-tech way to preserve food without setting up an industrial setup.

In this part, we go into more detail about these different types of freeze-drying tools. We explain how each key part works and fits into the whole process. We'll also walk you through the different options on the market, from cheap machines for home use to more complicated ones for businesses. With this information, you'll determine which freeze-drying setup fits your wants and goals the best.

Advancements in Freeze-Drying Technology:

Even though the basic ideas behind freeze-drying have mostly stayed the same over time, the technology and equipment used to do it have changed significantly. Because of these changes, the process works better, is easier to control, and can be used by more people.

In this part, we'll talk about some of these changes. There have been improvements in vacuum technology and heating systems, system automation and control, and scalable solutions that make freeze-drying processes more flexible and efficient.

They understand how freeze-drying is essential to get the most out of the process. Because of these new ideas and technological improvements, freeze-drying keeps improving, giving us more ways to use it than ever before.

Chapter 5
Troubleshooting and Maintenance

Understanding how freeze-drying works and how it works scientifically is only one part of the puzzle. This chapter looks at how to fix common problems, keep your freeze-drying tools in good shape, and improve or grow your freeze-drying business.

Common Issues in Freeze-Drying and How to Fix Them

Even if you do everything right, you may still have freeze-drying problems. Some common issues include the product taking too long to dry, drying unevenly, or drying too much or too little. Most of the time, these problems are caused by wrong temperature or vacuum level choices. So, it is crucial to know how to change these factors for the best drying results. This part will show you how to troubleshoot and fix these common problems so your freeze-drying process goes as smoothly as possible.

Maintenance of Your Freeze-Drying Machine

It is very important to keep your freeze-drying machine in good shape if you want it to last and work well. Regularly checking the vacuum and heating systems, seals, and other parts is a good idea. It's just as important to keep your machine clean. The leftovers can contaminate the next batch or make the vacuum and heat transfer less effective. This part will walk you through the recommended schedule for maintenance and show you the most important places to check and clean regularly.

Expanding and Improving Freeze-Drying Operations

Depending on your needs, you should consider improving your freeze-drying machine or adding more to what you do. Whether you're a homesteader who wants to save more of your harvests or a small business owner who wants to sell more products, knowing how to scale your freeze-drying processes is a handy skill. This section will show you what to consider when upgrading or growing your business, from picking the right equipment to scaling up your operations smartly.

This chapter's primary goal is to give you the information you need to keep your freeze-drying operations going well and to grow them to meet your needs. By knowing how to fix common problems, take care of your tools, and plan for upgrades or growth, you can continue to get the most out of this great way to store food.

Chapter 6
Quality Control in Freeze-Drying

Importance of Quality Control

During the freeze-drying process, you can't stress enough how important quality control is. It is very important to get the best product results, ensure customers are happy, and keep the freeze-drying method intact.

From a practical point of view, quality control in freeze-drying ensures that the food's nutrients, taste, structure, and color stay the same during the sublimation process. Proper quality control helps to keep the food's structure intact, which makes its shelf life much longer. This is very important because one of the main goals of freeze-drying is to make food last longer without hurting its quality.

Quality control is also key to ensuring the freeze-drying method works well and is safe. It means keeping an eye on the settings for freeze-drying, such as the temperature, the pressure, and the upkeep of the equipment. By keeping an eye on these factors, operational problems can be avoided, which protects both the freeze-dried product and the machinery used to make it.

From the consumer's point of view, good quality control is essential for building trust. People expect freeze-dried foods to taste good, recover well, and maintain nutritional value. Maintaining strict quality control practices ensures that freeze-dried goods always meet these standards, which builds the brand's image and the consumers' trust.

Also, quality control is important to follow the rules about food safety. It makes sure that the end freeze-dried product doesn't have any pathogens or other things that could be bad for your health. If you follow these standards, you can avoid potential health risks, fines from the government, and damage to your brand's image.

Overall, quality control in freeze-drying is important for more than just the end result. It's a very important step that controls the freeze-drying process and helps with operational efficiency, product quality, compliance with rules, and customer happiness.

Parameters to Monitor

During the freeze-drying process, several important factors must be carefully watched to make sure that the end product is safe and of good quality. Understanding and handling these factors well can help you avoid common problems with freeze-drying and make the process as effective and productive as possible.

Temperature: Temperature is one of the most important things to control during both the freezing and cooling steps. During freezing, the temperature must be kept low enough for the product to freeze fully. Then, during the drying phase, the temperature needs to be carefully controlled to help with sublimation and keep the product from getting damaged. It is important to keep an eye on the temperature inside the freeze-dryer so that the structure of the product doesn't fall apart or other temperature-related problems happen.

Pressure: Keeping the pressure inside the freeze-drying box low helps the sublimation process. Because the pressure is so low, the water in the frozen product can go straight from solid to gas. If the pressure is checked and changed often, the product won't "boil" or "melt," which could affect its quality and structure.

Drying Time: This is another important parameter that needs to be controlled because it directly affects the quality and speed of the freeze-drying process. The drying phase must go on until the desired amount of moisture is reached in the product. Over-drying can hurt the product's quality and taste, and under-drying can make it go bad faster because there is still wetness in it.

Wetness Content: The amount of wetness left in a freeze-dried product must be carefully watched because it greatly affects how stable the product is and how long it will last. Microbial growth can happen when there is too much leftover moisture, which shortens the product's shelf life. Because of this, the amount of wetness is usually kept as low as possible while still keeping the product's quality.

Performance of Equipment: It is important to keep an eye on the performance of the freeze-drying equipment, such as vacuum pumps, temperature monitors, and condenser units, on a regular basis to make sure the process goes smoothly. Equipment problems can stop the freeze-drying process and make the quality of the result less than it should be.

By closely monitoring these factors, manufacturers can successfully control the freeze-drying process. This improves the final product's quality and ensures the process works well. This care leads not only to better products but also to more customer trust and a better reputation for the brand.

Common Quality Issues and Solutions

During the freeze-drying process, there could be a number of quality problems, each of which needs a different kind of attention and action to fix. When you know about these common problems and use the right solutions, you improve the quality of the end product and make the whole process run more smoothly.

Collapse and shrinkage: One of the main problems with the quality of a freeze-dried product is that it can collapse or shrink. This usually happens when the temperature of the product during the first or second step of drying is higher than its collapse temperature. Solution: This can be avoided by keeping the product's temperature below its "collapse temperature" as it freeze-dries.

Not drying enough: If there is still moisture in a freeze-dried product, it can lead to the growth of microorganisms, which lowers the quality and shelf life of the product. Most of the time, this problem is caused by not enough drying time or bad process control. Solution: The time it takes to dry should be changed so that the ice completely melts. Regular moisture analysis can also help determine how much wetness is left and ensure the best drying is happening.

Drying in Different Ways: Sometimes, some parts of a product may be well-dried while other parts may not be. This makes the product dry in different ways. This can happen when the heat or load isn't spread out evenly. Solution: To get evenly dried goods, ensure the load is even and the heat is spread out evenly.

Oxidation: Some goods, especially those that are high in oils and fats, can go through oxidation when they are freeze-dried. This can change how they taste and how long they last. This problem can be solved by adding antioxidants or packing freeze-dried goods under a vacuum or in an inert atmosphere.

Darkening or changing the product's color: Enzymatic processes can cause some products, especially fruits, to get darker when they are freeze-dried. Solution: This can be stopped by using anti-browning agents or quickly freezing the product to slow down these enzymatic processes.

Damage to the Freeze-Drying Equipment: Problems like coil freezing up or vacuum leaks can damage and stop the process.

Regular maintenance and inspections of the equipment can help find and fix these problems before they become big problems.

By knowing about these common quality problems and how to fix them, manufacturers can fix problems and improve their freeze-drying process, making sure they make high-quality freeze-dried goods.

Chapter 7
The Rehydration Process in Freeze-Dried Foods

Rehydrating freeze-dried foods means restoring the water taken out during the freeze-drying process. When rehydrated properly, freeze-dried food returns to its original texture and taste. This is an important step for people who use freeze-dried items in their meals. This method is simple and works for many foods, including meats, fish, fruits, veggies, and even ready-made meals.

The Basic Rehydration Process

Rehydrating or reconstituting freeze-dried foods is an important part of using them. While freeze-drying takes almost all of the water out of foods, making them light and easy to store, rehydrating them brings them back to a more natural state, making them safe to eat.

1) Choose the right water. The water you use to rehydrate is very important. For the best benefits, you should use clean water that you can drink. The speed of recovery can be affected by the temperature of the water in a big way. Even though hot water can speed up the process, not all foods taste and feel better after being rehydrated with hot water. On the other hand, cold water takes longer but can keep some foods' shape and taste better.

2) Rehydration Ratio: Depending on the type of food, the amount of water needed to rehydrate will be different. Most of the time, the amount of dried product to water is similar, but this can change. For example, rice or pasta may need more water than other meals. Each type of food has different directions for how to rehydrate it.

3) Soaking Time: Getting water back into your body is not quick. When freeze-dried food gets wet, it takes the water and swells back up to its original size and texture. Depending on the food and the temperature of the water, this process can take anywhere from a few minutes to a couple of hours.

5) Draining: After rehydrating, you may need to drain some of the extra water. This is especially true for fruits and veggies. After being drained, these foods are ready to eat or used in recipes just like fresh versions.

6) Cooking and seasoning: Some freeze-dried foods need to be cooked before they can be eaten. Rehydrating them is only the first step. Also, the freeze-drying process can take away some of the food's taste, so it's often best to add seasonings after rehydration.

Rehydrating food is a simple process, but knowing how it works for different kinds of food can make a big difference in how it tastes and feels. One can get the most out of freeze-dried foods by controlling the type and temperature of the water, the rehydration ratio, the resting time, and the steps after rehydration, such as draining, cooking, and seasoning.

Rehydration of Different Food Types

The process of rehydrating is very different for each kind of food. To get the best results from recovery, you must understand these details and keep in mind that temperature and time have a big effect on the outcome. Here is a more in-depth look at how long it takes for different food groups to rehydrate:

Veggies: Most freeze-dried veggies rehydrate quickly, taking about 5-10 minutes in hot water (near boiling point, around 95-100°C) and 10-20 minutes in cold water. Most of the time, two parts water to one part veggie works best. Draining the extra water after soaking is important to keep the taste from diluting.

Fruits: Cold water (around 15-20°C) is best for rehydrating fruits because it helps keep their natural colors and tastes. Most of the time, the same amount of water and fruit is used to rehydrate. Apples and pears with more fiber might need a little more water. Most fruits get wet again in 10–20 minutes, but heavier fruits may take up to 30 minutes.

Meat and fish: Most freeze-dried meats and seafood need hot water (around 75-80°C) to be rehydrated. This could take anywhere from 5 minutes to 15 minutes, depending on how thick the slices are. You may need to heat or boil the mixture for a full re-mix. Usually, there is one part of the meat for every two parts of water, but this could change based on the type and cut of meat.

Ready-made meals and dishes with many ingredients: To rehydrate ready-made meals, you usually need hot water (around 80-85°C). Since these meals have more than one ingredient, the time it takes to rehydrate can be anywhere from 10 to 30 minutes. The amount of water to food would vary on the dish but is usually between 1 and 2 parts water to 2 parts food.

Herbs and spices: Freeze-dried herbs and spices can often be used in cooking without rehydrating first. But if you want to refresh them, you should only soak them for a few minutes in a small amount of luke-warm water (30–35°C).

Grains and legumes: Grains and legumes are the hardest to rehydrate. They usually need hot water (around 100°C) and as much as a 3:1 water-to-grain ratio. The process of rehydrating can take anywhere from 10 minutes (for small grains like quinoa) to 20–30 minutes (for bigger grains and legumes).

It's important to remember that these are just suggestions, and the exact rehydration factors can change based on the food and your own taste. When freeze-dried foods are rehydrated the right way, they get as close as possible to their original texture, taste, and nutritional value.

Factors Affecting the Rehydration Process

The process of rehydrating freeze-dried foods is complicated and depends on a number of things that affect how close the food gets to its original state. Here, we'll talk about these factors in more depth:

1. Water Temperature: The speed and efficiency of rehydrating depend a lot on the temperature of the water used. Hot water, usually between 80 and 100°C, helps the body absorb water faster, which speeds up the healing process. But it's important to remember that delicate things like fruits might lose color and flavor at high temperatures so lukewarm water might be better.

2. Size and shape of food pieces: The time it takes to rehydrate freeze-dried food is directly related to its size and shape. Smaller or thinner cut pieces have more surface area for their size so they can absorb water faster. On the other hand, bigger pieces or things with more complicated shapes may take longer. By cutting the food into thin slices or small chunks before freeze-drying, you can make it much easier to rehydrate.

3. Soaking Time: The amount of time the food spends in water is also important. Most freeze-dried foods need between 5 and 20 minutes to get back to their original state. But it's important not to soak them too long, which could make them soggy and lose their structure.

4. pH Level: The refreshing process can be slightly changed by how acidic or alkaline the water is. Most foods do well with a neutral pH (around 7), but fruits and veggies might do better in slightly acidic conditions, which can help keep their color and flavor.

5. The amount of salt: The salt in the food or in the water used to rehydrate can greatly affect how well you rehydrate. Salt can soak up some of the water, leaving less for the food to use and slowing down the process. This is something to consider for foods or meals with salt or spices added.

6. Stirring: A light stir can speed up the rehydration process by helping the water flow around and into the food pieces. But too much shaking could hurt the food, especially if it is fragile, and cause it to lose its shape and structure.

7. The temperature of the food: The process can also be affected by the temperature of the food before it is rehydrated. Food that has been kept at room temperature will get wet faster than food that has been kept cold or frozen. Freeze-dried food should be kept at room temperature and rehydrated at the same temperature for best results.

Understanding and controlling these factors can improve rehydrating freeze-dried foods, bringing them as close as possible to their original texture, taste, and nutritional value.

Breakfast

Freeze-Dried Berry and Yogurt Parfait

Preparation Time: 15 minutes | Cooking Time: 0 minutes | Portion Size: 1 serving

Ingredients:

- 1 cup freeze-dried mixed berries
- 1 cup Greek yogurt
- 2 tablespoons honey
- 1/4 cup granola
- Fresh berries (optional, for garnish)

Instructions:

1) In a bowl, combine the freeze-dried mixed berries and Greek yogurt.

2) Drizzle honey over the mixture and stir until well combined.

3) Take a serving glass or bowl and start layering the parfait. Begin with a spoonful of the yogurt and berry mixture, followed by a sprinkle of granola. Repeat the layers until you have used up all the ingredients.

4) Finish the parfait with a final dollop of the yogurt and berry mixture on top.

5) Garnish with fresh berries for an extra pop of color and flavor if desired.

6) Place the parfait in the freezer for 10 minutes to chill and set.

Nutrition Data:

Calories: 350 | Protein: 18g | Carbohydrates: 65g | Dietary Fiber: 7g | Sugar: 43g | Fat: 5g | Saturated Fat: 1g | Sodium: 80mg | Potassium: 420mg

Overnight Oats with Freeze-Dried Fruits

Preparation Time: 5 minutes | Cooking Time: 0 minutes | Portion Size: 1 serving

Ingredients:

- 1/2 cup rolled oats
- 1/2 cup milk (dairy or plant-based)
- 1 tablespoon chia seeds
- 1 tablespoon honey or maple syrup
- 1/4 teaspoon vanilla extract
- 1/4 cup freeze-dried fruits (such as strawberries, blueberries, or raspberries)
- 1 tablespoon nuts or seeds (optional for topping)

Instructions:

1) Combine the rolled oats, milk, chia seeds, honey (maple syrup), and vanilla extract in a jar or container. Stir well to make sure all of the ingredients are mixed well. mixed.

2) Add the freeze-dried fruits to the oat mixture and gently stir to distribute them evenly.

3) Seal the jar (container) with a lid. Refrigerate overnight or for at least 4 hours, allowing the oats to soften and absorb the flavors.

4) Now it time to serve, give the oats a good stir. If you want to, you can add a splash of milk to achieve your preferred consistency.

5) Top the overnight oats with nuts or seeds for added crunch and texture.

6) Enjoy your delicious and convenient overnight oats with freeze-dried fruits!

Nutrition Data:

Calories: 300 | Protein: 9g | Carbohydrates: 47g | Dietary Fiber: 9g | Sugar: 16g | Fat: 8g | Saturated Fat: 1g | Sodium: 60mg | Potassium: 310mg

Freeze-Dried Smoothie Bowl

Preparation Time: 10 minutes | Cooking Time: 0 minutes | Portion Size: 1 serving

Ingredients:

- 1 frozen banana
- 1/2 cup frozen berries (strawberries, blueberries, or raspberries)
- 1/2 cup Greek yogurt
- 1/4 cup milk (dairy or plant-based)
- 1 tablespoon honey or maple syrup
- 1/4 cup freeze-dried fruits (such as mango, pineapple, or banana)
- Toppings of your choice (fresh fruits, nuts, seeds, coconut flakes, etc.)

Instructions:

1) Combine the frozen banana, frozen berries, Greek yogurt, milk, and honey or maple syrup in a blender.

2) Blend until smooth and creamy. If needed, add more milk to achieve your desired consistency.

3) Pour the smoothie into a bowl.

4) Sprinkle the freeze-dried fruits on top of the smoothie.

5) Add toppings that you like, such as fresh fruits, nuts, seeds, or coconut flakes.

6) Enjoy your delicious and nutritious freeze-dried smoothie bowl!

Nutrition Data:

Calories: 350 | Protein: 15g | Carbohydrates: 67g | Dietary Fiber: 10g | Sugar: 40g | Fat: 5g | Saturated Fat: 2g | Sodium: 80mg | Potassium: 770mg

Healthy Pancakes with Freeze-Dried Berries

Preparation Time: 10 minutes | Cooking Time: 15 minutes | Portion Size: 2 servings

Ingredients:

- 1 cup whole wheat flour
- 1 tablespoon baking powder
- 1 tablespoon honey or maple syrup
- 1/2 teaspoon vanilla extract
- 1 cup milk (dairy or plant-based)
- 1 egg
- 1/4 cup freeze-dried berries (such as strawberries, blueberries, or raspberries)
- Cooking spray or butter for greasing

Instructions:

1) Whisk together wheat flour and baking powder in a bowl.

2) Grub a separate mixing bowl, and whisk together the honey or maple syrup, vanilla extract, milk, and egg until well combined.

3) Now combined the wet ingredients into the dry ingredients. do not overmix; just a few lumps are fine.

4) Gently fold in the freeze-dried berries, ensuring they are evenly distributed throughout the batter.

5) Heat a non-stick pan or griddle (medium heat). Apply a thin layer of cooking or oil spray or butter to the surface.

6) Using a 1/4 cup, and pour the pancake batter onto the skillet, spacing them apart.

7) Cook until bubbles form on the surface of the pancakes and the edges start to look set, about 2-3 minutes.

8) Then flip the pancakes and cook for 1-2 minutes or until golden brown.

9) Moved the cooked pancakes to a plate and cover it to keep them warm.

10) Repeat steps 6-9 with the remaining batter.

11) Last step serve the pancakes with toppings, such as fresh berries, yogurt, or a drizzle of honey.

Nutrition Data:

Calories: 220 | Protein: 8g | Carbohydrates: 42g | Dietary Fiber: 6g | Sugar: 10g | Fat: 3g | Saturated Fat: 1g | Sodium: 400mg | Potassium: 350mg

Homemade Muesli with Freeze-Dried Fruits and Nuts

Preparation Time: 10 minutes | Cooking Time: 0 minutes | Portion Size: 1 serving

Ingredients:

- 1/2 cup rolled oats
- 1 tablespoon chia seeds
- 1 tablespoon flaxseeds
- 1 tablespoon unsweetened coconut flakes
- 2 tablespoons freeze-dried fruits (such as strawberries, blueberries, or apples)
- 2 tablespoons mixed nuts, chopped (such as almonds, walnuts, or cashews)
- 1 tablespoon honey or maple syrup
- 1/2 cup milk (dairy or plant-based)
- Fresh fruits, yogurt, or additional milk, for serving (optional)

Instructions:

1) Combine the rolled oats, chia seeds, flaxseeds, and unsweetened coconut flakes in a mixing bowl.

2) Add the freeze-dried fruits and mixed nuts to the bowl, and stir until well-mixed.

3) Drizzle the honey (maple syrup) over the mixture, and stir again to distribute the sweetener evenly.

4) Pour the milk into a mixing bowl, and stir until all the ingredients are coated and well combined. The mixture will become moist but not soggy.

5) Let the muesli sit for about 5 minutes to allow the flavors to meld together and the oats to soften slightly.

6) Serve the muesli as is or personalize it by adding fresh fruits, yogurt, or a splash of additional milk.

7) Enjoy your homemade muesli with freeze-dried fruits and nuts!

Nutrition Data:

Calories: 380 | Protein: 12g | Carbohydrates: 45g | Dietary Fiber: 10g | Sugar: 16g | Fat: 18g | Saturated Fat: 4g | Sodium: 60mg | Potassium: 540mg

Protein-Packed Quinoa Porridge with Freeze-Dried Fruits

Preparation Time: 5 minutes | Cooking Time: 20 minutes | Portion Size: 2 servings

Ingredients:

- 1/2 cup quinoa
- 1 cup water
- 1 cup milk (dairy or plant-based)
- 2 tablespoons protein powder (vanilla or unflavored)
- 1 tablespoon honey or maple syrup
- 1/4 teaspoon cinnamon
- 1/4 cup freeze-dried fruits (such as strawberries, blueberries, or peaches)
- 2 tablespoons chopped nuts or seeds (such as almonds, pumpkin seeds, or chia seeds)
- Fresh fruits or additional toppings, for serving (optional)

Instructions:

1) Rinse the quinoa under cold water to remove any bitterness.
2) In a saucepan, combine the rinsed quinoa and water. Bring to a boil over medium heat.
3) Lower the heat, cover the saucepan, and let it cook for about 15 to 20 minutes, or until the quinoa is soft and the liquid has been absorbed.
4) Once the quinoa is cooked, take the pan off the heat and let it sit for 5 minutes with the lid on.
5) In a separate small pot, heat the milk over medium heat until it is warm. Make sure it doesn't boil.
6) Stir in the protein powder, honey or maple syrup, and cinnamon into the warm milk until well combined.
7) Pour the protein milk mixture over the cooked quinoa and stir to combine.
8) Gently fold in the freeze-dried fruits and chopped nuts or seeds.
9) Divide the quinoa porridge into serving bowls.
10) If desired, top the porridge with fresh fruits or additional toppings of your choice.
11) Serve the protein-packed quinoa porridge warm and enjoy!

Nutrition Data:

Calories: 350 | Protein: 20g | Carbohydrates: 45g | Dietary Fiber: 6g | Sugar: 12g | Fat: 10g | Saturated Fat: 2g | Sodium: 90mg | Potassium: 450mg

Avocado Toast with Freeze-Dried Tomatoes

Preparation Time: 5 minutes | Cooking Time: 0 minutes | Portion Size: 1 serving

Ingredients:

- 1 avocado
- 2 slices of whole grain bread
- 1 tablespoon lemon juice
- Salt and pepper, to taste
- 2 tablespoons freeze-dried tomatoes
- Red pepper flakes (optional, for garnish)

Instructions:

1) Slice in half the avocado, remove the seed, and scoop the flesh into a bowl.

2) Add lemon juice to the bowl with the avocado.

3) Using a fork, mash the avocado and lemon juice together until you reach your desired consistency.

4) Season with salt and pepper the mashed avocado to taste.

5) Toast the slices of whole grain bread until they are golden and crispy.

6) Spread the mashed avocado evenly onto the toasted bread slices.

7) Sprinkle the freeze-dried tomatoes over the avocado spread.

8) If desired, garnish with a sprinkle of red pepper flakes for added heat and flavor.

9) Serve the avocado toast immediately and enjoy!

Nutrition Data:

Calories: 250 | Protein: 7g | Carbohydrates: 28g | Dietary Fiber: 10g | Sugar: 2g | Fat: 15g | Saturated Fat: 2g | Sodium: 200mg | Potassium: 600mg

Vegan Chia Pudding with Freeze-Dried Mango

Preparation Time: 5 minutes | Cooking Time: 4 hours (Chilling Time) | Portion Size: 2 servings

Ingredients:

- 1/4 cup chia seeds
- 1 cup milk plant-based (such as almond milk, coconut milk, or soy milk)
- 1 tablespoon maple syrup or agave nectar
- 1/2 teaspoon vanilla extract
- 1/4 cup freeze-dried mango
- Fresh mango slices, for garnish (optional)

Instructions:

1) In a bowl, combine the chia seeds, plant-based milk, maple syrup or agave nectar, and vanilla extract.

2) Whisk the mixture vigorously for a couple of minutes until the chia seeds are evenly dispersed.

3) Let the mixture sit for 5 minutes, then whisk again to break up any clumps that may have formed.

4) Cover the bowl and refrigerate the chia pudding for at least 4 hours or overnight to allow it to thicken and set.

5) Once the chia pudding has thickened to your desired consistency, remove it from the refrigerator.

6) Stir in the freeze-dried mango, ensuring it is evenly distributed throughout the pudding.

7) Spoon the vegan chia pudding into serving glasses or bowls.

8) If desired, garnish with fresh mango slices for an extra burst of flavor and texture.

9) Serve the chia pudding chilled and enjoy!

Nutrition Data:

Calories: 180 | Protein: 6g | Carbohydrates: 20g | Dietary Fiber: 12g | Sugar: 5g | Fat: 8g | Saturated Fat: 1g | Sodium: 60mg | Potassium: 320mg

Whole Grain Muffins with Freeze-Dried Blueberries

Preparation Time: 15 minutes | Cooking Time: 20 minutes | Portion Size: 12 muffins

Ingredients:

- 2 cups whole wheat flour
- 1/2 cup rolled oats
- 1/2 cup coconut sugar or others
- 2 teaspoons baking powder
- 1/2 teaspoon baking soda
- 1/2 teaspoon salt
- 1 teaspoon ground cinnamon
- 1 cup unsweetened applesauce
- 1/4 cup coconut oil, melted
- 1/4 cup almond milk or others
- 1 teaspoon vanilla extract
- 1 cup freeze-dried blueberries

Instructions:

1) Preheat the oven to 375°F (190°C). Grease a muffin tin or line it with paper liners.

2) In a large mixing bowl, whisk together the whole wheat flour, rolled oats, coconut sugar or (brown sugar) and ground cinnamon.

3) Mix the unsweetened applesauce, melted coconut oil, almond milk, and vanilla flavor in a separate bowl. Mix well until all the liquid items are well blended.

4) Add in a mixing bowl all the wet and dry ingredients. Do not overmix; chunks are acceptable.

5) Gently fold in the freeze-dried blueberries, ensuring they are evenly distributed throughout the batter.

6) Place the batter into the muffin tin that has been made, filling each cup about 3/4 of the way.

7) Bake for 18–20 minutes, or until a toothpick put into the middle of a muffin comes out clean.

8) Take the muffin pan out of the oven and give the muffins a few minutes to cool down.

Nutrition Data:

Calories: 180 | Protein: 3g | Carbohydrates: 29g | Dietary Fiber: 4g | Sugar: 11g | Fat: 6g | Saturated Fat: 4g | Sodium: 200mg | Potassium: 160mg

Egg Scramble with Freeze-Dried Veggies

Preparation Time: 5 minutes | Cooking Time: 10 minutes | Portion Size: 2 servings

Ingredients:

- 4 large eggs
- 1/4 cup milk
- Salt and pepper, to taste
- 1/4 cup freeze-dried vegetables (such as bell peppers, onions, or spinach)
- 1 tablespoon olive oil or cooking spray
- Fresh herbs or shredded cheese, for garnish (optional)

Instructions:

1) In a bowl, whisk together the eggs and milk until well combined. Season with salt and pepper to taste.

2) Stir the freeze-dried veggies into the egg mixture to make sure they are spread out evenly.

3) Over medium heat, heat olive oil or cooking spray in a pan that doesn't stick.

4) Pour the egg mixture into the skillet and let it cook undisturbed for a few seconds until it begins to set around the edges.

5) Using a spatula, gently stir and scramble the eggs, incorporating the vegetables as you go.

6) Keep cooking and turning the eggs until they are the way you like them.

7) Take the pan off the heat and put the scrambled eggs on a plate to serve.

8) If desired, garnish with fresh herbs or shredded cheese for added flavor and presentation.

9) Serve the egg scramble hot and enjoy!

Nutrition Data:

Calories: 220 | Protein: 16g | Carbohydrates: 2g | Dietary Fiber: 0g | Sugar: 1g | Fat: 16g | Saturated Fat: 4g | Sodium: 220mg | Potassium: 180mg

Snacks

Freeze-Dried Tropical Fruit Salad

Preparation Time: 10 minutes | Cooking Time: 0 minutes | Portion Size: 2 servings

Ingredients:

- 1 cup freeze-dried tropical fruits (such as mango, pineapple, papaya, or coconut)
- 1 cup fresh mixed tropical fruits (such as kiwi, banana, or dragon fruit), diced
- 1 tablespoon lime juice
- 1 tablespoon honey or maple syrup (optional)
- Fresh mint leaves, for garnish (optional)

Instructions:

1) In a bowl, combine the freeze-dried tropical fruits and fresh mixed tropical fruits.

2) Drizzle lime juice over the fruits for a tangy flavor.

3) If you want more sugar, you can add honey or maple syrup. Change the amount depending on how much you like.

4) Gently toss all the ingredients together until the freeze-dried fruits are rehydrated, and the flavors are well combined.

5) Give the fruit salad a few minutes to sit so the tastes can mix.

6) Use fresh mint leaves as a garnish for a fresh taste and a pop of color.

7) Serve the freeze-dried tropical fruit salad as a light and delightful snack or as a side dish to complement a main meal.

Nutrition Data:

Calories: 100 | Protein: 1g | Carbohydrates: 25g | Dietary Fiber: 3g | Sugar: 18g | Fat: 1g | Saturated Fat: 0g | Sodium: 0mg | Potassium: 200mg

Crunchy Freeze-Dried Veggie Chips

Preparation Time: 10 minutes | Cooking Time: 2 hours | Portion Size: Varies

Ingredients:

- Assorted vegetables of your choice (such as carrots, beets, zucchini, or sweet potatoes)
- Olive oil
- Salt and pepper, to taste

Instructions:

1) Preheat your oven to 200°F (95°C) or the lowest temperature setting available.

2) Wash and dry the vegetables thoroughly. Slice them into thin, uniform rounds or strips. It's best to use a mandoline or a sharp knife for even slices.

3) Place the vegetable slices in a bowl and drizzle with a small amount of olive oil, tossing gently to coat each slice.

4) Place the vegetable slices that have been sprayed in a single layer on a baking sheet that has been lined with parchment paper.

5) Add salt and pepper over the vegetable slices to taste.

6) Put the baking sheet in an oven that has already been heated, and leave the oven door slightly open so that liquid can escape.

7) Bake the vegetable slices for approximately 2 hours or until they become crispy and dry. Check them periodically to prevent burning.

8) Take the baking sheet out of the oven and wait until the chips are totally cool to touch.

9) Once cooled, the veggie chips are ready to be enjoyed as a healthy and crunchy snack!

Nutrition Data:

Calories: Varies | Protein: Varies | Carbohydrates: Varies | Dietary Fiber: Varies | Sugar: Varies | Fat: Varies | Saturated Fat: Varies | Sodium: Varies | Potassium: Varies

Protein-Packed Greek Yogurt with Freeze-Dried Berries

Preparation Time: 5 minutes | Cooking Time: 0 minutes | Portion Size: 1 serving

Ingredients:

- 1 cup Greek yogurt
- 1/4 cup freeze-dried berries (such as strawberries, blueberries, or raspberries)
- 1 tablespoon honey or maple syrup
- 1 tablespoon chia seeds or flaxseeds (optional)
- 1 tablespoon nuts or granola for topping (optional)

Instructions:

1) In a bowl, spoon the Greek yogurt.

2) Add the freeze-dried berries to the yogurt.

3) Drizzle honey or maple syrup over the yogurt and berries.

4) If desired, sprinkle chia seeds or flaxseeds on top for added nutrition.

5) Stir all the ingredients together until the freeze-dried berries are evenly distributed.

6) Top the yogurt with nuts or granola for some added crunch and texture.

7) Enjoy your protein-packed Greek yogurt with freeze-dried berries as a delicious and nutritious snack or breakfast option!

Nutrition Data:

Calories: 200 | Protein: 15g | Carbohydrates: 20g | Dietary Fiber: 3g | Sugar: 13g | Fat: 7g | Saturated Fat: 1g | Sodium: 60mg | Potassium: 230mg

Freeze-Dried Apple and Almond Butter Sandwiches

Preparation Time: 5 minutes | Cooking Time: 0 minutes | Portion Size: 1 serving

Ingredients:

- 2 slices of whole-grain bread
- 2 tablespoons almond butter
- 1/4 cup freeze-dried apple slices
- 1 teaspoon honey or maple syrup (optional)

Instructions:

1) Take the two slices of whole grain bread and spread almond butter evenly on one side of each slice.

2) Arrange the freeze-dried apple slices on one slice of bread, covering the almond butter completely.

3) If you like, drizzle honey or maple syrup over the freeze-dried apple pieces if you want to add more sweetness.

4) Place the other slice of bread, almond butter side down, on top of the apple slices to form a sandwich.

5) Gently press the sandwich together to ensure it holds together.

6) Enjoy your freeze-dried apple and almond butter sandwich as a delicious and nutritious snack or meal!

Nutrition Data:

Calories: 350 | Protein: 10g | Carbohydrates: 45g | Dietary Fiber: 10g | Sugar: 10g | Fat: 16g | Saturated Fat: 2g | Sodium: 220mg | Potassium: 420mg

Spiced Chickpea Crunchies with Freeze-Dried Spinach

Preparation Time: 10 minutes | Cooking Time: 25 minutes | Portion Size: 4 servings

Ingredients:

- 2 cans of chickpeas, drained and rinsed
- 2 tablespoons olive oil
- 1 tablespoon freeze-dried spinach powder
- 1 teaspoon ground cumin
- 1 teaspoon paprika
- 1/2 teaspoon garlic powder
- 1/2 teaspoon salt
- 1/4 teaspoon cayenne pepper (optional for heat)

Instructions:

1) Turn your oven on and heat it to 400°F (200°C).

2) Rinse and drain the chickpeas, then use a cooking towel or paper towels to pat them dry.

3) In a bowl, combine the dried chickpeas, olive oil, freeze-dried spinach powder, cumin, paprika, garlic powder, salt, and cayenne pepper (if using). Mix well to ensure the chickpeas are evenly coated with the spices.

4) Spread the chickpeas that have been seasoned in a single layer on the baking sheet that has been ready.

5) Bake the chickpeas in an oven that has been warm for 20 to 25 minutes or until they are golden brown and crispy. Halfway through the cooking time, stir them to ensure they brown evenly.

6) Once the chickpeas are done, remove them from the oven and set them on the baking sheet to cool.

7) Once cooled, the spiced chickpea crunchies are ready to enjoy as a healthy and flavorful snack!

Nutrition Data:

Calories: 180 | Protein: 8g | Carbohydrates: 25g | Dietary Fiber: 6g | Sugar: 2g | Fat: 6g | Saturated Fat: 1g | Sodium: 300mg | Potassium: 250mg

Peanut Butter Energy Balls with Freeze-Dried Raspberries

Preparation Time: 15 minutes | Cooking Time: 0 minutes | Portion Size: 12 energy balls

Ingredients:

- 1 cup rolled oats
- 1/2 cup peanut butter
- 1/4 cup honey or maple syrup
- 1/4 cup freeze-dried raspberries
- 1/4 cup chia seeds/ground flaxseeds
- 1/4 cup dark chopped chips (optional)
- 1/2 teaspoon vanilla extract
- Pinch of salt

Instructions:

1) Mix the rolled oats, peanut butter, honey or maple syrup, freeze-dried raspberries, chia seeds or ground flaxseeds, tiny dark chocolate chips (if using), vanilla, and a pinch of salt in a bowl.

2) Mix all the ingredients together until well combined. The mixture should be sticky and hold together when pressed.

3) Put the lid on the bowl and put the mixture in the fridge for about 15 minutes. This will make rolling into balls easily.

4) After chilling, take small portions of the mixture and roll them between your palms to form bite-sized energy balls.

5) Repeat the rolling process until all of the mixture is used.

6) Keep the energy balls in the fridge for up to a week in a jar that keeps air out.

7) Enjoy the peanut butter energy balls as a quick and nutritious snack or as a pre-or post-workout boost!

Nutrition Data:

Calories: 140 | Protein: 4g | Carbohydrates: 16g | Dietary Fiber: 3g | Sugar: 8g | Fat: 7g | Saturated Fat: 1g | Sodium: 50mg | Potassium: 120mg

Freeze-Dried Edamame and Quinoa Salad

Preparation Time: 15 minutes | Cooking Time: 15 minutes | Portion Size: 4 servings

Ingredients:

- 1 cup quinoa
- 2 cups water or vegetable broth
- 1 cup freeze-dried edamame
- 1/2 cup diced cucumber
- 1/2 cup diced bell pepper
- 1/4 cup chopped red onion
- 1/4 cup chopped fresh cilantro
- 2 tablespoons lemon juice
- 2 tablespoons olive oil
- 1 tablespoon Dijon mustard
- Salt and pepper, to taste

Instructions:

1) Rinse the quinoa thoroughly under cold water to remove any bitterness.

2) In a saucepan, combine the rinsed quinoa and water or vegetable broth. Bring to a boil.

3) Turn the heat down to low, cover the pan, and let the quinoa boil for about 15 minutes, or until the liquid is absorbed and the quinoa is soft. Use a fork to fluff the quinoa, and then let it cool.

4) Mix the cooked and cooled quinoa, freeze-dried edamame, cucumber, bell pepper, chopped red onion, and chopped fresh cilantro in a big bowl.

5) In a different bowl, whisk together the lemon juice, olive oil, Dijon mustard, pepper, and salt.

6) Add the dressing over the quinoa mixture and toss to coat everything evenly.

7) Try and season as you like, adding more salt and pepper if needed.

8) Let the salad marinate in the refrigerator for not less than 30 minutes before serving to allow the flavors to meld together.

9) Serve the freeze-dried edamame and quinoa salad as a refreshing and nutritious side dish or a light lunch option.

Nutrition Data:

Calories: 240 | Protein: 10g | Carbohydrates: 30g | Dietary Fiber: 6g | Sugar: 3g | Fat: 10g | Saturated Fat: 1g | Sodium: 180mg | Potassium: 380mg

Sweet and Spicy Freeze-Dried Mango Salsa

Preparation Time: 10 minutes | Cooking Tim: 0 minutes | Portion Size: 4 servings

Ingredients:

- 1 cup freeze-dried mango, diced
- 1/2 cup diced red bell pepper
- 1/4 cup diced red onion
- 1/4 cup chopped fresh cilantro
- 1 jalapeño pepper, seeds removed and finely chopped
- 1 tablespoon lime juice
- 1 tablespoon honey or maple syrup
- 1/2 teaspoon ground cumin
- Salt, to taste

Instructions:

1) In a bowl, combine the freeze-dried mango, diced red bell pepper, diced red onion, chopped fresh cilantro, and finely chopped jalapeño.

2) In a different mixing bowl, whisk together the lime juice, honey or maple syrup, ground cumin, and salt.

3) Add the dressing over the mango and gently incorporate all the ingredients.

4) Control if the seasoning is how you like it by adding more salt or lime juice.

5) Let the salsa rest for a few minutes to allow the flavors to meld together.

6) Serve the sweet and spicy freeze-dried mango salsa as a zesty and vibrant accompaniment to tortilla chips, grilled meats, fish, or tacos.

Nutrition Data:

Calories: 60 | Protein: 1g | Carbohydrates: 15g | Dietary Fiber: 2g | Sugar: 12g | Fat: 0g | Saturated Fat: 0g | Sodium: 90mg | Potassium: 160mg

Freeze-Dried Vegetable Hummus Dip

Preparation Time: 10 minutes | Cooking Time: 0 minutes | Portion Size: 6 servings

Ingredients:

- 1 can (15 ounces) chickpeas (garbanzo beans), drained and rinsed
- 1/4 cup tahini
- 2 tablespoons lemon juice
- 2 tablespoons olive oil
- 1 clove garlic, minced
- 1/2 teaspoon ground cumin
- 1/2 teaspoon salt
- 1/4 teaspoon paprika
- 1/4 teaspoon cayenne pepper (optional for heat)
- 1/4 cup freeze-dried vegetables (such as bell peppers, carrots, or peas)

Instructions:

1) Combine in the blender, chickpeas, tahini, lemon juice, olive oil, minced garlic, ground cumin, salt, paprika, and cayenne pepper (if using). Blend until smooth and creamy.

2) Add the freeze-dried vegetables to the processor or blender and pulse a few times to incorporate them into the hummus. This will give the dip a burst of vegetable flavor and add some texture.

3) If the hummus appears too thick, you can add a bit of water or additional olive oil to achieve your desired consistency.

4) Try the hummus and adjust the seasoning as needed, adding more salt or lemon juice if desired.

5) Transfer the freeze-dried vegetable hummus dip to a serving bowl.

6) Serve the hummus with an array of fresh vegetables, pita bread, or tortilla chips for dipping.

Nutrition Data:

Calories: 160 | Protein: 6g | Carbohydrates: 16g | Dietary Fiber: 5g | Sugar: 2g | Fat: 9g | Saturated Fat: 1g | Sodium: 270mg | Potassium: 240mg

Spicy Roasted Chickpeas with Freeze-Dried Seasonings

Preparation time: 5 minutes | Cooking time: 40 minutes | Portion size: 4 servings

Ingredients:

- 1 can (15 ounces) chickpeas, drained and rinsed
- 1 tablespoon olive oil
- 1 teaspoon smoked paprika
- 1/2 teaspoon chili powder
- 1/2 teaspoon garlic powder
- 1/4 teaspoon cayenne pepper (adjust to taste)
- Salt to taste

Instructions:

1) Set your oven to 400°F (200°C) and put parchment paper on a baking sheet.

2) Put in a kitchen towel the chickpeas and pat them dry with your hands to remove any extra water.

3) Combine In a bowl the chickpeas, olive oil, smoked paprika, chili powder, garlic powder, cayenne pepper, and salt. Toss the chickpeas well with the spices.

4) Spread on the baking sheet the seasoned chickpeas.

5) Once the oven is preheated, roast in the oven for 30-40 minutes, or until the chickpeas are crispy and golden brown, stirring them halfway through the cooking time for even browning.

6) Remove from the oven and let the chickpeas cool completely before serving.

Nutrition data (per serving):

Calories: 150/200 | Protein: 6-8g | Carbohydrates: 20-25g | Dietary Fiber: 5-7g | Sugar: 2-4g | Fat: 5-7g | Saturated Fat: 0.5-1mg |

Lunch

Freeze-Dried Vegetable Stir Fry with Tofu

Preparation Time: 15 minutes | Cooking Time: 15 minutes | Portion Size: 4 servings

Ingredients:

- 1 package (14 ounces) of firm tofu
- 2 tablespoons soy sauce
- 1 tablespoon sesame oil

2 cloves garlic, minced

- 1 teaspoon grated ginger
- 1 cup freeze-dried vegetables
- 1 tablespoon vegetable oil
- 1/2 cup sliced mushrooms
- 1/2 cup sliced onions
- 1/2 cup sliced bell peppers
- 1/2 cup sliced carrots
- 1/2 cup sliced zucchini
- 2 tablespoons oyster sauce
- 1 tablespoon cornstarch
- 1/4 cup water
- Cooked rice or noodles for serving

Instructions:

1) To remove extra moisture, drain the tofu and press it between paper towels or a clean dish towel. Cut the tofu into cubes or slices.

2) Whisk the soy sauce, sesame oil, chopped garlic, and grated ginger in a bowl. Put the tofu cubes in the bowl and gently stir them so the sauce covers them. Set aside to marinate for about 10 minutes.

3) While the tofu is marinating, rehydrate the freeze-dried vegetables by placing them in a bowl and adding enough hot water to cover them. Let them sit for a few minutes until they have softened. Drain and place away.

4) Start heating the vegetable oil in a large pan or wok over medium-high heat. Add the marinated tofu cubes to the skillet and cook until they are golden brown and crispy all around. Remove it from the skillet and place it aside.

5) Use the same skillet to add the sliced mushrooms, onions, bell peppers, carrots, and zucchini. Stir-fry the vegetables for a few minutes until they are crisp-tender.

6) Whisk together in a bowl the oyster sauce, cornstarch, and water until smooth. Then add the sauce mixture into the skillet with the vegetables and stir to coat everything evenly. Cook until the sauce thickens.

7) Add the rehydrated freeze-dried vegetables and the cooked tofu to the skillet. Gently combine all the ingredients and heat everything through.

8) Remove from heat and serve the freeze-dried vegetable with tofu over cooked rice or noodles.

Nutrition Data:

Calories: 280 | Protein: 17g | Carbohydrates: 22g | Dietary Fiber: 4g | Sugar: 6g | Fat: 15g | Saturated Fat: 2g | Sodium: 700mg | Potassium: 500mg

Salmon Salad with Freeze-Dried Citrus Dressing

Preparation Time: 15 minutes | Cooking Time: 12 minutes | Portion Size: 2 servings

Ingredients:

- For the Salmon:

- 2 salmon fillets (about 6 ounces each)
- 1 tablespoon olive oil
- Salt and pepper, to taste
- For the Freeze-Dried Citrus Dressing:
- 1/4 cup freeze-dried citrus powder (such as lemon or orange)
- 2 tablespoons olive oil
- 1 tablespoon honey or maple syrup
- 1 tablespoon white wine vinegar or apple cider vinegar
- 1 clove garlic, minced
- Salt and pepper, to taste

- For the Salad:

- 4 cups mixed salad greens
- 1/2 cup cherry tomatoes, halved
- 1/4 cup sliced red onions
- 1/4 cup crumbled feta cheese
- 2 tablespoons fresh herbs chopped (such as parsley or basil)

Instructions:

1) Turn your oven on and heat it to 400°F (200°C). Put parchment paper on a baking sheet.

2) Place the salmon fillets on the cookie sheet or baking sheet that has been set up. Add the olive oil over them and add salt and pepper to taste.

3) Bake the salmon in the preheated oven for about 12 minutes or until cooked through and flaky. Take it out of the oven and let it cool down a bit.

4) Meanwhile, prepare the freeze-dried citrus dressing. In a small bowl, whisk together the freeze-dried citrus powder, olive oil, honey or maple syrup, vinegar, minced garlic, salt, and pepper. Place away to let the flavors mix.

5) In a big bowl, combine the mixed salad greens, cherry tomatoes, sliced red onions, crumbled feta cheese, and chopped fresh herbs.

6) Break the cooked salmon into bite-sized pieces and add them to the salad bowl.

7) Distribute the freeze-dried citrus dressing over the salad, and then gently toss the salad to mix the dressing with all the vegetables.

8) Divide the salmon salad into two plates or bowls.

9) Serve the salmon salad with freeze-dried citrus dressing as a delicious and nutritious main course.

Nutrition Data:

Calories: 400 | Protein: 28g | Carbohydrates: 20g | Dietary Fiber: 4g | Sugar: 14g | Fat: 23g | Saturated Fat: 5g | Sodium: 450mg | Potassium: 900mg

Spiced Chicken and Freeze-Dried Vegetable Soup

Preparation Time: 15 minutes | Cooking Time: 30 minutes | Portion Size: 4 servings

Ingredients:

- 2 tablespoons olive oil
- 1 onion, diced
- 2 cloves garlic, minced
- 2 carrots, diced
- 2 celery stalks, diced
- 1 teaspoon ground cumin
- 1 teaspoon paprika
- 1/2 teaspoon ground turmeric
- 1/2 teaspoon ground coriander
- 1/4 teaspoon cayenne pepper (optional for heat)
- 4 cups chicken or vegetable broth
- 2 cups water
- 2 cups freeze-dried mixed vegetables (such as corn, peas, and green beans)
- 2 cups cooked chicken, shredded
- Salt and pepper, to taste
- Fresh cilantro or parsley for garnish (optional)

Instructions:

1) Start heating the olive oil in a big pot. Once reach medium heat, Add onion, and garlic (chopped) and cook until the onion is clear and smells good.

2) Add the carrots and celery (diced) to the pot and continue to sauté for a few minutes until the vegetables start to soften.

3) Stir in the ground cumin, paprika, turmeric, coriander, and cayenne pepper (if using). Cook for a few minutes to toast the spices and enhance their flavors.

4) Pour the chicken or veggie broth with water inside the pot and bring the mixture to a boil.

5) Reduce to low the heat, cover the top of the pot, and let the soup simmer for 15 minutes to allow the flavors to meld together.

6) Stir in the freeze-dried mixed vegetables and cooked chicken. Simmer for another 10 minutes or until the vegetables have rehydrated and the chicken is heated through.

7) Season to taste the soup with salt and pepper. Adjust the seasoning as needed.

8) Ladle the spiced chicken and freeze-dried vegetable soup into bowls and garnish with fresh cilantro or parsley, if desired.

9) Serve the soup hot and enjoy the comforting flavors of this hearty dish.

Nutrition Data:

Calories: 250 | Protein: 20g | Carbohydrates: 18g | Dietary Fiber: 4g | Sugar: 6g | Fat: 10g | Saturated Fat: 2g | Sodium: 800mg | Potassium: 600mg

Beef Stroganoff with Freeze-Dried Mushrooms

Preparation Time: 10 minutes | Cooking Time: 25 minutes | Portion Size: 4 servings

Ingredients:

- 1 pound beef sirloin or tenderloin, thinly sliced
- 2 tablespoons olive oil
- 1 onion, thinly sliced
- 2 cloves garlic, minced
- 1 cup freeze-dried mushrooms
- 1 cup beef broth
- 1 tablespoon Worcestershire sauce
- 1 tablespoon Dijon mustard
- 1 cup sour cream
- Salt and pepper, to taste
- Cooked egg noodles or rice for serving
- Chopped fresh parsley for garnish (optional)

Instructions:

1)   In a large pan (skillet), heat the olive oil over medium-high heat. Add the thinly sliced beef and cook until browned on all sides. Remove the beef from the skillet and set it aside.

2)   Use the same pan (skillet), and add the thinly sliced onion and minced garlic. Sauté until the onion becomes translucent and fragrant.

3)   Add the freeze-dried mushrooms to the skillet and cook for a few minutes until they have rehydrated and become tender.

4)   Return the cooked beef to the skillet with the mushrooms and onions.

5)   Mix the beef broth into the pan in the Dijon mustard and Worcestershire sauce. Get the mixture to a low boil.

6)   Reduce the heat to low and stir in the sour cream. Cook for a few minutes, stirring occasionally, until the sauce is heated through. Be careful not to let the sauce boil, or the sour cream may separate from it.

7)   Season the beef stroganoff with salt and pepper to taste. Adjust the seasoning as needed.

8)   Serve the beef stroganoff over cooked egg noodles or rice. Garnish with chopped fresh parsley, if desired.

9)   Enjoy the comforting and flavorful beef stroganoff with freeze-dried mushrooms and onions.

Nutrition Data:

Calories: 400 | Protein: 30g | Carbohydrates: 12g | Dietary Fiber: 2g | Sugar: 5g | Fat: 26g | Saturated Fat: 10g | Sodium: 600mg | Potassium: 700mg

Quinoa Salad with Freeze-Dried Beets and Avocado

Preparation Time: 15 minutes | Cooking Time: 15 minutes | Portion Size: 4 servings

Ingredients:

- 1 cup quinoa
- 2 cups water or vegetable broth
- 1 cup freeze-dried beets
- 1 ripe avocado, diced
- 1/2 cup diced cucumber
- 1/4 cup chopped red onion
- 1/4 cup chopped fresh parsley
- 2 tablespoons lemon juice
- 2 tablespoons olive oil
- Salt and pepper, to taste

Instructions:

1) Rinse the quinoa thoroughly under cold water to remove any bitterness.

2) In a saucepan, combine the rinsed quinoa and water or vegetable broth. Bring to a boil.

3) Turn the heat down to low, cover the pan, and let the quinoa boil for about 15 minutes, or until the liquid is absorbed and the quinoa is soft. Use a fork to fluff the quinoa, and then let it cool down.

4) Now Combine in a mixing bowl the cooked and cooled quinoa, rehydrated and chopped freeze-dried beets, diced avocado, diced cucumber, chopped red onion, and chopped fresh parsley.

5) In a different small bowl, mix the lemon juice, olive oil, salt, and pepper together with a whisk.

6) After pouring the dressing over the quinoa mixture, gently toss everything together so that it coats each component evenly.

7) Taste the food and add more salt and pepper, if you want, to make it taste better.

8) Let the salad in the fridge for at least 30 minutes before serving it so the tastes can blend.

9) Serve the vegan quinoa salad with freeze-dried beets and avocado as a refreshing and nutritious side dish or a light meal option.

Nutrition Data:

Calories: 280 | Protein: 8g | Carbohydrates: 35g | Dietary Fiber: 8g | Sugar: 5g | Fat: 14g | Saturated Fat: 2g | Sodium: 160mg | Potassium: 580mg

Shrimp Paella with Freeze-Dried Peas and Bell Peppers

Preparation Time: 15 minutes | Cooking Time: 40 minutes | Portion Size: 4 servings

Ingredients:

- 2 tablespoons olive oil
- 1 onion, diced
- 2 cloves garlic, minced
- 1 red bell pepper, diced
- 1 yellow bell pepper, diced
- 1 cup Arborio rice (or other)
- 1 teaspoon smoked paprika
- 1/2 teaspoon turmeric
- 1/2 teaspoon saffron threads
- 2 cups vegetable broth
- 1 can (14 ounces) diced tomatoes
- 1 cup freeze-dried peas, rehydrated
- 1 pound shrimp, peeled and deveined
- Salt and pepper, to taste
- Lemon wedges for serving
- Fresh parsley, for garnish (optional)

Instructions:

1) Start heating the olive oil over medium heat in a big pan or paella pan.

2) Add the first two ingredients, onion, and garlic (chopped), and cook over medium heat until the onion turns clear and smells good.

3) Add the diced red bell pepper and yellow bell pepper to the skillet and cook for a few minutes until they start to soften.

4) Stir in the Arborio rice, smoked paprika, turmeric, and saffron threads (if using). Toast for a few minutes rice and spices, stirring constantly.

5) Pour the water from the vegetables into the pan and mix in the diced tomatoes. Heat the mixture until it boils.

6) Turn the heat down to low, cover the pan, and let the paella boil for about 20 minutes until the rice is almost done and most of the liquid has been absorbed.

7) Stir in the rehydrated freeze-dried peas and arrange the shrimp on top of the rice.

8) Cover the skillet again and cook for another 10 minutes or less, until the shrimp are cooked through, and the rice is fully tender.

9) Season the shrimp paella with salt and pepper to taste. Adjust the seasoning as needed.

10) Remove the skillet from the heat and let the paella rest for a few minutes before serving.

11) Serve the shrimp paella with freeze-dried peas and bell peppers. Add on the side some lemon wedges. Garnish with fresh parsley, if desired.

Nutrition Data:

Calories: 380 | Protein: 25g | Carbohydrates: 45g | Dietary Fiber: 6g | Sugar: 8g | Fat: 10g | Saturated Fat: 2g | Sodium: 800mg | Potassium: 650mg

Turkey Chili with Freeze-Dried Corn and Tomatoes

Preparation Time: 15 minutes | Cooking Time: 45 minutes | Portion Size: 6 servings

Ingredients:

- 1 tablespoon olive oil
- 1 onion, diced
- 2 cloves garlic, minced
- 1 pound ground turkey
- 1 can (14 ounces) diced tomatoes
- 1 can (14 ounces) tomato sauce
- 1 cup freeze-dried corn, rehydrated
- 1 can (14 ounces) of kidney beans
- 1 can (14 ounces) of black beans
- 2 tablespoons chili powder
- 1 teaspoon ground cumin
- 1/2 teaspoon paprika
- 1/2 teaspoon dried oregano
- Salt and pepper, to taste
- Optional toppings: shredded cheese, sour cream, chopped green onions

Instructions:

1) To heat the olive oil, place it in a big saucepan or Dutch oven and set the temperature to medium.

2) When the onion is transparent, and the garlic has taken on a fragrant flavor, it is done sautéing. Throw in some onions and garlic.

3) Add the ground turkey to the pot and heat it until it is browned and cooked, breaking it up with a wooden spoon if possible.

4) Stir in the diced tomatoes, tomato sauce, rehydrated freeze-dried corn, kidney beans, black beans, chili powder, ground cumin, paprika, dried oregano, salt, and pepper.

5) Bring to a boil, immediately lower the heat to a low setting, cover, and continue to simmer the chili for thirty minutes while stirring it occasionally.

6) Season it to your taste.

7) Serve the turkey chili hot, garnished with your preferred toppings such as shredded cheese, sour cream, or chopped green onions.

8) Enjoy the flavorful and hearty turkey chili with freeze-dried corn and tomatoes.

Nutrition Data:

Calories: 320 | Protein: 25g | Carbohydrates: 35g | Dietary Fiber: 10g | Sugar: 7g | Fat: 10g | Saturated Fat: 2.5g | Sodium: 800mg | Potassium: 900mg

Pork Stir Fry with Freeze-Dried Pineapple and Broccoli

Preparation Time: 20 minutes | Cooking Time: 15 minutes | Portion Size: 4 servings

Ingredients:

- 1 pound pork tenderloin, thinly sliced
- 2 tablespoons soy sauce
- 2 tablespoons hoisin sauce
- 1 tablespoon cornstarch
- 1/2 teaspoon ground ginger
- 1/4 teaspoon garlic powder
- 2 tablespoons vegetable oil
- 1 onion, thinly sliced
- 2 cloves garlic, minced
- 1 cup freeze-dried pineapple, rehydrated and chopped
- 2 cups broccoli florets
- 1 red bell pepper, thinly sliced
- 1/4 cup low-sodium chicken broth or water
- Salt and pepper, to taste
- Cooked rice for serving

Instructions:

1) Mix the soy sauce, hoisin sauce, cornstarch, ground ginger, and garlic powder in a bowl. Add the pork slices and stir everything together to cover everything. Marinate for 10 minutes before serving.

2) Warm the vegetable oil in a pan (skillet) or wok over medium heat.

3) Add the marinated pork to the skillet and stir-fry for about 4-5 minutes, or until the pork is cooked through and nicely browned. Remove the pork from the pan (skillet) and set it aside.

4) Use the same pan (skillet), add the sliced onion and minced garlic. Stir-fry for a couple of minutes until the onion becomes translucent and fragrant.

5) Add the rehydrated and chopped freeze-dried pineapple, broccoli florets, and sliced red bell pepper to the skillet. Stir-fry for about 3-4 minutes or until the vegetables are tender-crisp.

6) Return the cooked pork to the skillet and pour in the low-sodium chicken broth or water. Stir-fry for another minute or until everything is well combined and heated through.

7) Season the stir-fry with salt and pepper to taste. Adjust the seasoning as needed.

8) Serve the pork stir fry with freeze-dried pineapple and broccoli over cooked rice.

9) Garnish with some green onions (optional), and enjoy the delightful flavors of this stir-fry dish.

Nutrition Data:

Calories: 350 | Protein: 25g | Carbohydrates: 30g | Dietary Fiber: 4g | Sugar: 12g | Fat: 12g | Saturated Fat: 3g | Sodium: 650mg | Potassium: 750mg

Freeze-Dried Black Bean and Corn Burritos

Preparation time: 15 minutes | Cooking time: 15 minutes | Portion size: 4 servings

Ingredients:

- 1 cup freeze-dried black beans
- 1 cup freeze-dried corn kernels
- 1 small onion, diced
- 2 cloves garlic, minced
- 1 teaspoon cumin powder
- 1 teaspoon chili powder
- Salt and pepper to taste
- 1 cup water
- 4 large flour tortillas
- Optional toppings: shredded lettuce, diced tomatoes, sliced avocado, salsa, sour cream, cilantro

Instructions:

1) Rehydrate the freeze-dried black beans and corn according to the package instructions. Typically, you'll need to soak them in water for a few minutes until they become tender. Drain and set aside.

2) Put a spoonful of oil in a pan and warm it over medium heat. Sauté the onion and garlic until they are transparent, then add them to the pan.

3) Add the rehydrated black beans and corn to the skillet. Stir in the cumin powder, chili powder, salt, and pepper. Cook for a few minutes to allow the flavors to meld together.

4) Pour in the water and bring the mixture to a simmer. Let it cook for about 10 minutes until the excess liquid evaporates and the beans and corn are fully cooked.

5) Warm the flour tortillas in a dry skillet or in the microwave until pliable.

6) Spoon the black bean and corn mixture onto each tortilla, dividing it equally among them. Add any desired toppings, such as shredded lettuce, diced tomatoes, sliced avocado, salsa, sour cream, or cilantro.

7) Fold the sides of the tortillas inward, then roll them up tightly to form the burritos.

8) Serve the burritos warm and enjoy!

Nutrition data:

Calories: 320 | Protein: 11g | Carbohydrates: 58g | Dietary Fiber: 10g | Sugar: 3g | Fat: 5g | Saturated Fat: 1g | Sodium: 310mg | Potassium: 610mg

Chicken Shawarma Wraps with Freeze-Dried Cucumbers

Preparation time: 20 minutes | Cooking time: 15 minutes | Portion size: 4 wraps

Ingredients:

- 1 pound boneless, skinless chicken breasts
- 2 tablespoons olive oil
- 2 tablespoons lemon juice
- 2 cloves garlic, minced
- 1 teaspoon ground cumin
- 1 teaspoon ground paprika
- 1 teaspoon ground coriander
- 1/2 teaspoon ground turmeric
- Salt and pepper to taste
- 4 large tortilla wraps
- 1 cup freeze-dried cucumbers
- 1 cup freeze-dried tomatoes
- 1/2 cup Greek yogurt
- Fresh parsley or cilantro, chopped (for garnish)

Instructions:

1) Olive oil, lemon juice, minced garlic, cumin, paprika, coriander, turmeric, salt, and pepper should all be mixed in a bowl. Use this combined mixture as a marinade.

2) Thinly slice the chicken breasts and put them in the marinate. Make sure the chicken is well coated. Let it marinate for at least 15 minutes, or refrigerate for up to 2 hours for more flavor.

3) Heat a skillet over medium-high heat. Add the marinated chicken strips and cook until they are golden brown and cooked through, about 6-8 minutes.

4) While the chicken is cooking, rehydrate the freeze-dried cucumbers and tomatoes according to the package instructions. Typically, you'll need to soak them in water for a few minutes until they become rehydrated. Drain and set aside.

5) Warm the tortilla wraps in a dry skillet or in the microwave until pliable.

6) Spread a tablespoon of Greek yogurt on each tortilla to make the wraps. Add a portion of the cooked chicken, followed by the rehydrated cucumbers and tomatoes.

7) Sprinkle some fresh parsley or cilantro on top for added freshness and flavor.

8) Roll up the wraps tightly, folding in the sides as you go.

9) Serve the chicken shawarma wraps immediately and enjoy!

Nutrition data:

Calories: 350 | Protein: 28g | Carbohydrates: 28g | Dietary Fiber: 4g | Sugar: 5g | Fat: 14g | Saturated Fat: 2g | Sodium: 350mg | Potassium: 580mg

Chicken Alfredo with Sun-Dried Tomatoes and Spinach

Preparation Time: 15 minutes | Cooking Time: 25 minutes | Portion Size: 4 servings

Ingredients:

- 8 ounces fettuccine pasta
- 2 boneless, skinless chicken breasts, sliced
- 2 tablespoons olive oil
- 4 cloves garlic, minced
- 1 cup heavy cream
- 1 cup grated Parmesan cheese
- 1 cup freeze-dried spinach, rehydrated
- 1/2 cup sun-dried tomatoes, chopped
- Salt and pepper, to taste
- Fresh parsley, for garnish (optional)

Instructions:

1) Read the directions on the package to cook the fettuccine until it is al dente. Drain and put away.

2) In a large pan (skillet), heat the olive oil over medium heat.

3) Add the sliced chicken breasts to the skillet and season with salt and pepper. Cook for about 5-6 minutes per side or until cooked through and no longer pink in the center. Once the chicken is done, remove it from the pan.

4) After removing the chicken, use the same skillet to cook the minced garlic for about 1 minute until fragrant.

5) Pour the heavy cream and turn the heat down to a boil. Heat for two to three minutes, stirring occasionally.

6) Stir in the grated Parmesan cheese and keep cooking for another 2–3 minutes or until the sauce has thickened.

7) Add the rehydrated freeze-dried spinach and chopped sun-dried tomatoes to the skillet. Stir well to combine.

8) Return the cooked chicken to the skillet and toss it with the sauce and vegetables. Cook for another 2–3 minutes to make sure everything is hot.

9) Season the sauce with salt and pepper based on your taste if needed.

10) Add the cooked fettuccine pasta to the skillet and toss it with the sauce and chicken until well coated.

11) Divide the chicken Alfredo pasta with freeze-dried spinach and sun-dried tomatoes among the plates.

12) Serve the plate hot with some garnish with fresh parsley.

Nutrition Data:

Calories: 580 | Protein: 38g | Carbohydrates: 40g | Dietary Fiber: 4g | Sugar: 4g | Fat: 32g | Saturated Fat: 15g | Sodium: 720mg | Potassium: 600mg

Beef & Vegetable Skewers with Bell Peppers and Onions

Preparation Time: 20 minutes | Cooking Time: 15 minutes | Portion Size: 4 servings

Ingredients:

- 1 pound beef sirloin
- 1 red bell pepper
- 1 green bell pepper
- 1 yellow bell pepper
- 1 red onion
- 2 tablespoons olive oil
- 2 cloves garlic, minced
- 1 teaspoon paprika
- 1 teaspoon dried oregano
- 1/2 teaspoon dried thyme
- Salt and pepper, to taste

Instructions:

1) Soaking wooden skewers in water for 30 minutes will stop them from catching fire.

2) Set the grill or pan to medium-high heat and let it warm up.

3) In a kitchen bowl, combine the olive oil, minced garlic, paprika, dried oregano, dried thyme, salt, and pepper. Mix well to make a marinade.

4) Add the beef sirloin cubes to the marinade and toss until well-coated. Let it marinate for at least 10 minutes or up to 1 hour in the refrigerator.

5) Thread the marinated beef cubes onto the soaked wooden skewers, alternating with the bell pepper pieces and onion chunks.

6) Place the skewers on the preheated grill or pan and cook for about 3-4 minutes per side, or until the beef is cooked to your desired doneness and the vegetables are tender-crisp.

7) Remove the skewers from the grill and let them rest for a few minutes before serving.

8) Serve the beef and vegetable skewers with freeze-dried bell peppers and onions as a delicious and flavorful meal.

Nutrition Data:

Calories: 280 | Protein: 24g | Carbohydrates: 10g | Dietary Fiber: 3g | Sugar: 5g | Fat: 16g | Saturated Fat: 4g | Sodium: 100mg | Potassium: 660mg

Vegan Pad Thai with Freeze-Dried Tofu and Bean Sprouts

Preparation time: 20 minutes | Cooking time: 15 minutes | Portion size: 2 servings

Ingredients:

- 6 ounces of rice noodles
- 2 tablespoons vegetable oil
- 1/2 cup freeze-dried tofu, rehydrated and sliced
- 1/2 cup freeze-dried bean sprouts, rehydrated
- 1/4 cup freeze-dried green onions, rehydrated and chopped
- 2 cloves garlic, minced

- 2 tablespoons soy sauce
- 1 tablespoon tamarind paste
- 1 tablespoon maple syrup or agave nectar
- 1 tablespoon lime juice
- 1/4 teaspoon red pepper flakes
- Crushed peanuts (optional, for garnish)
- Fresh cilantro (optional for garnish)
- Lime wedges (optional for serving)

Instructions:

1) Follow the directions on the package to make the rice noodles. Drain and put away.

2) Heat the vegetable oil over medium heat in a big pan or wok. Add the rehydrated tofu slices and cook for about 3–4 minutes until they are golden brown and crispy. Take the tofu out of the pan and put it on a plate.

3) Add to the pan chopped garlic to the same pan and cook for about 30 seconds or until the garlic starts to smell good. Stir-fry for another 2 minutes after adding the bean sprouts and green onions that have been soaked in water.

4) Whisk the soy sauce, tamarind paste, maple syrup or agave nectar, lime juice, and red pepper flakes in a small bowl.

5) Push the bean sprouts and green onions to one side of the skillet. Pour the sauce into the empty side of the skillet and let it simmer for a minute or two until heated through.

6) Add the cooked rice noodles and crispy tofu to the skillet. Toss everything together until well coated with the sauce. Cook for an additional 2-3 minutes until the noodles are heated through.

7) Take it off the heat and, if you want, top it with crushed peanuts and fresh parsley.

8) Serve the vegan Pad Thai hot with lime wedges on the side.

Nutrition data:

Calories: 380 | Protein: 12g | Carbohydrates: 60g | Dietary Fiber: 4g | Sugar: 9g | Fat: 10g | Saturated Fat: 1g | Sodium: 900mg | Potassium: 380mg

Seafood Gumbo with Freeze-Dried Okra and Shrimp

Preparation Time: 30 minutes | Cooking Time: 90 minutes | Portion Size: 6 servings

Ingredients:

- 1/2 cup vegetable oil
- 1/2 cup all-purpose flour
- 1 onion, diced
- 1 green bell pepper, diced
- 2 celery stalks, diced
- 4 cloves garlic, minced
- 1 can (14 ounces) diced tomatoes
- 4 cups vegetable or seafood broth
- 1 cup freeze-dried okra, rehydrated
- 1 pound shrimp, peeled and deveined
- 1/2 pound crabmeat
- 1 tablespoon Cajun seasoning
- 1 teaspoon dried thyme
- 1 teaspoon dried oregano
- 1 bay leaf
- Salt and pepper, to taste
- Cooked white rice for serving
- Fresh parsley, for garnish (optional)

Instructions:

1) Use a pot or Dutch oven to heat the vegetable oil over medium heat.

2) Add the all-purpose flour to the pot and stir continuously to make a roux. Cook the roux, turning it often, until it turns a dark brown like chocolate. This can take 15 to 20 minutes.

3) Add the chopped onion, green bell pepper, celery, and crushed garlic when the roux is the color you want. Stir well so that the roux covers the veggies. Cook for about 5 minutes or until the vegetables have softened.

4) Mix in the diced tomatoes and cook for another 2 minutes.

5) Slowly pour in the vegetable or seafood broth, stirring continuously to avoid any lumps. Bring the mixture to a boil.

6) Reduce the heat to low and add the rehydrated freeze-dried okra, shrimp, crabmeat, Cajun seasoning, dried thyme, dried oregano, bay leaf, salt, and pepper. Stir well to combine.

7) Cover the pot and let the gumbo simmer for about 1 hour, stirring occasionally.

8) Taste the gumbo and adjust the seasoning with salt and pepper if needed.

9) Remove the bay leaf before serving.

10) To serve, spoon a portion of cooked white rice into individual bowls and ladle the seafood gumbo over the rice.

11) Garnish with fresh parsley, if desired.

Nutrition Data:

Calories: 350 | Protein: 20g | Carbohydrates: 20g | Dietary Fiber: 4g | Sugar: 4g | Fat: 22g | Saturated Fat: 3g | Sodium: 800mg | Potassium: 500mg

Turkey Meatballs with Freeze-Dried Cranberries and Sag

Preparation Time: 20 minutes | Cooking Time: 25 minutes | Portion Size: 4 servings

Ingredients:

- 1 pound ground turkey
- 1/2 cup breadcrumbs
- 1/4 cup grated Parmesan cheese
- 1/4 cup freeze-dried cranberries
- 1/4 cup finely chopped onion
- 2 cloves garlic, minced
- 1 tablespoon chopped fresh sage
- 1 egg
- 1/4 teaspoon black pepper
- 1 can (14 ounces) diced tomatoes
- 1 can (8 ounces) tomato sauce
- 2 cloves garlic, minced
- 1 teaspoon dried basil
- 1 teaspoon dried oregano
- 1/2 teaspoon sugar

Instructions:

1) Preheat the oven to 400°F (200°C). Put parchment paper or a little bit of oil on a baking sheet.

2) In a large bowl, combine the ground turkey, breadcrumbs, grated Parmesan cheese, rehydrated and chopped freeze-dried cranberries, finely chopped onion, minced garlic, chopped fresh sage, egg, salt, and black pepper. Mix well until all the ingredients are evenly incorporated.

3) Make meatballs with the mixture that are about 1 inch in diameter and put them on the baking sheet that has been prepared. About 20 meatballs should come out of this.

4) Bake the meatballs in the preheated oven for about 20-25 minutes or until they are cooked through and browned.

5) Make the sauce while the meatballs are in the oven. In a saucepan, combine the diced tomatoes, tomato sauce, minced garlic, dried basil, dried oregano, sugar, salt, and pepper. Stir well to combine.

6) Cook the sauce at a low simmer for about 10 minutes, stirring regularly, over medium heat.

7) Once the meatballs are cooked, transfer them to the saucepan with the sauce. Gently toss the meatballs in the sauce to coat them evenly.

8) Let the meatballs and sauce blend for another 5 minutes while simmering.

9) Serve the turkey meatballs with freeze-dried cranberries and sage with pasta, rice, or crusty bread, and garnish with additional chopped sage if desired.

Nutrition Data:

Calories: 320 | Protein: 28g | Carbohydrates: 21g | Dietary Fiber: 4g | Sugar: 8g | Fat: 13g | Saturated Fat: 4g | Sodium: 890mg | Potassium: 690mg

Lamb Tagine with Freeze-Dried Apricots and Chickpeas

Preparation Time: 20 minutes | Cooking Time: 150 minutes | Portion Size: 4 servings

Ingredients:

- 2 pounds lamb shoulder
- 2 tablespoons olive oil
- 1 onion, diced
- 3 cloves garlic, minced
- 1 teaspoon ground cumin
- 1 teaspoon ground coriander
- 1 teaspoon ground cinnamon
- 1/2 teaspoon ground ginger
- 1/4 teaspoon ground turmeric
- 1/4 teaspoon cayenne pepper
- 1 can (14 ounces) diced tomatoes
- 2 cups vegetable or chicken broth
- 1 cup freeze-dried apricots, rehydrated and halved
- 1 can (14 ounces) chickpeas, drained and rinsed

Instructions:

1) Olive oil should be cooked in a big pot or tagine with a heavy bottom over medium heat. Cook the lamb cubes on all sides until they are cooked. Remove the lamb from the stew and set it aside.

2) Once add the diced onion and minced garlic to the same pot. Sauté the onion until it is soft and transparent.

3) Add the ground cumin, ground coriander, ground cinnamon, ground ginger, ground turmeric, and cayenne pepper (if using) to the pot. Stir well so that the spices cover the onions and garlic. Cook for an additional 1-2 minutes to toast the spices and release their flavors.

4) Return the browned lamb cubes to the pot. Stir in the diced tomatoes and vegetable or chicken broth. Season with salt and pepper to taste.

5) Raise the temperature until the liquid boils, then lower it to a simmer. Simmer for about 2 hours with the lid on or until the lamb is soft and the flavors have blended.

6) Add the rehydrated and halved freeze-dried apricots and drained chickpeas to the pot. Stir well to combine. To give the flavors time to meld and the apricots time to soften, cover and continue simmering for another 30 minutes.

7) Add salt and pepper if necessary.

8) Serve the lamb tagine with freeze-dried apricots and chickpeas over cooked couscous or rice. Garnish with chopped fresh cilantro, if desired.

Nutrition Data:

Calories: 420 | Protein: 30g | Carbohydrates: 32g | Dietary Fiber: 6g | Sugar: 18g | Fat: 18g | Saturated Fat: 6g | Sodium: 860mg | Potassium: 960mg

Tofu and Bamboo Shoots Vegan Thai Green Curry

Preparation Time: 15 minutes | Cooking Time: 25 minutes | Portion Size: 4 servings

Ingredients:

- 2 tablespoons vegetable oil
- 2 tablespoons Thai green curry paste
- 1 can (13.5 ounces) of coconut milk
- 1 cup vegetable broth
- 1 red bell pepper, sliced
- 1 green bell pepper, sliced
- 1 cup sliced bamboo shoots
- 1 cup freeze-dried tofu, rehydrated and sliced
- 1 cup snap peas
- 1 tablespoon soy sauce or tamari
- 1 tablespoon lime juice
- 1 tablespoon brown sugar or coconut sugar
- Fresh basil leaves, for garnish
- Cooked rice or noodles for serving

Instructions:

1) Put the oil in a big pan or wok and heat it over medium heat. Stir-frying something for a minute or so will bring out the flavors of the Thai green curry paste you just added.

2) Add the veggie broth and coconut milk. Stir well to combine the curry paste with the liquids. Bring the mixture to a simmer.

3) Add bell peppers sliced, bamboo shoots, rehydrated and sliced freeze-dried tofu, and snap peas to the skillet. Stir to coat the vegetables and tofu with the curry sauce.

4) Simmer the curry for about 15 minutes or until the vegetables are tender and the flavors have melded together.

5) Stir in the soy sauce or tamari, lime juice, and brown sugar. Adjust the seasonings to taste.

6) Remove the skillet from the heat.

7) Serve the vegan Thai green curry with freeze-dried tofu and bamboo shoots over cooked rice or noodles. Garnish with fresh basil leaves, if desired.

Nutrition Data:

Calories: 280 | Protein: 8g | Carbohydrates: 20g | Dietary Fiber: 5g | Sugar: 8g | Fat: 20g | Saturated Fat: 15g | Sodium: 520mg | Potassium: 480mg

Crab Cakes with Freeze-Dried Corn and Red Bell Pepper

Preparation Time: 20 minutes | Cooking Time: 10 minutes | Portion Size: 4 servings

Ingredients:

- 1 pound lump crab meat
- 1/2 cup freeze-dried corn, rehydrated and drained
- 1/4 cup diced red bell pepper
- 1/4 cup mayonnaise
- 2 tablespoons chopped fresh parsley
- 2 tablespoons bread crumbs
- 1 egg, lightly beaten
- 1 tablespoon Dijon mustard
- 1 teaspoon Old Bay seasoning
- Salt and pepper, to taste
- 2 tablespoons vegetable oil

Instructions:

1)   In a large bowl, gently combine the lump crab meat, rehydrated and drained freeze-dried corn, diced red bell pepper, mayonnaise, chopped fresh parsley, bread crumbs, lightly beaten egg, Dijon mustard, Old Bay seasoning, salt, and pepper. The crab meat should not be pulverized too much.

2)   Make 8 individual crab cakes from the ingredients by dividing them evenly. After forming the crab cakes, place them on a baking sheet covered in foil or paper and chill in the fridge for 30 minutes.

3)   In a large pan (skillet), melt the vegetable oil over moderate heat.

4)   Carefully place the crab cakes in the skillet and cook for about 4-5 minutes on each side or until they are golden brown and heated through.

5)   Take the crab cakes out of the pan and place them on a paper towel to soak up any remaining oil.

6)   Serve the crab cakes with a side of tartar sauce or aioli, and enjoy!

Nutrition Data:

Calories: 240 | Protein: 20g | Carbohydrates: 8g | Dietary Fiber: 1g | Sugar: 1g | Fat: 14g | Saturated Fat: 2g | Sodium: 620mg | Potassium: 320mg

Caesar Salad with Freeze-Dried Romaine and Croutons

Preparation Time: 15 minutes | Cooking Time: 15 minutes | Portion Size: 4 servings

Ingredients:

- For the Salad:

- 2 boneless, skinless chicken breasts
- Salt and pepper, to taste
- 1 tablespoon olive oil
- 4 cups freeze-dried romaine lettuce, rehydrated and drained
- 1/2 cup freeze-dried croutons
- 1/4 cup grated Parmesan cheese

- For the Dressing:

- 1/4 cup mayonnaise
- 2 tablespoons lemon juice
- 1 tablespoon Dijon mustard
- 2 cloves garlic, minced
- 1/4 cup grated Parmesan cheese
- Salt and pepper, to taste

Instructions:

1) Salt and pepper the chicken breasts. Use a pan to heat the Olive oil over medium heat. The chicken needs to be cooked for around 6-8 minutes per side. Take it away from the stove and let it sit for a while. Make chicken strips with a sharp knife.

2) In a large bowl, combine the rehydrated and drained freeze-dried romaine lettuce, freeze-dried croutons, and grated Parmesan cheese.

3) In a separate small bowl, whisk together the mayonnaise, lemon juice, Dijon mustard, minced garlic, grated Parmesan cheese, salt, and pepper to make the dressing.

4) Mix the romaine lettuce with the sliced chicken. The salad is ready when the dressing is poured over it and gently mixed.

5) Divide the salad into four plates or bowls.

6) Serve the chicken Caesar salad with freeze-dried romaine and croutons immediately, and enjoy!

Nutrition Data:

Calories: 320 | Protein: 24g | Carbohydrates: 12g | Dietary Fiber: 2g | Sugar: 2g | Fat: 20g | Saturated Fat: 5g | Sodium: 600mg | Potassium: 500mg

Lentil Soup with Freeze-Dried Carrots and Celery

Preparation Time: 15 minutes | Cooking Time: 1 hour | Portion Size: 6 servings

Ingredients:

- 1 cup dried green lentils
- 2 tablespoons olive oil
- 1 onion, chopped
- 2 cloves garlic, minced
- 2 carrots, diced
- 2 stalks of celery, diced
- 1 can (14.5 ounces) diced tomatoes
- 4 cups vegetable broth
- 1 bay leaf
- 1 teaspoon dried thyme
- 1 teaspoon ground cumin
- Salt and pepper, to taste
- 1/2 cup freeze-dried carrots
- 1/2 cup freeze-dried celery
- Fresh parsley, for garnish (optional)

Instructions:

1) Rinse the dried green lentils under cold water and drain them. Set aside.

2) Use the pot to heat the olive oil over medium heat. Add the chopped onion and minced garlic. Sauté until the onion becomes translucent and the garlic becomes fragrant.

3) Proceed to add the diced carrots and celery to the pot. Cook for a few minutes until the vegetables start to soften.

4) Pour in the diced tomatoes, vegetable broth, bay leaf, dried thyme, and ground cumin. Stir well to combine.

5) Season the soup, adding saol or pepper to taste. Bring the mixture to a boil.

6) Bring to a boil, then turn the heat down to low, cover, and let cook for 45 minutes to an hour or until the lentils are soft.

7) Stir in the freeze-dried carrots and celery. Cook for an additional 5 minutes to rehydrate the vegetables.

8) Remove the bay leaf from the soup.

9) Ladle the lentil soup into bowls. Garnish with fresh parsley, if desired.

10) Serve the lentil soup with freeze-dried carrots and celery hot, and enjoy!

Nutrition Data:

Calories: 220 | Protein: 12g | Carbohydrates: 35g | Dietary Fiber: 14g | Sugar: 6g | Fat: 4g | Saturated Fat: 0.5g | Sodium: 650mg | Potassium: 870mg

Dinner

Freeze-Dried Vegetable Ratatouille with Grilled Chicken

Preparation Time: 20 minutes | Cooking Time: 40 minutes | Portion Size: 4 servings

Ingredients:

- For the Ratatouille:

- 2 tablespoons olive oil
- 1 onion, sliced
- 2 cloves garlic, minced
- 1 eggplant, diced
- 1 zucchini, diced
- 1 yellow bell pepper, diced
- 1 red bell pepper, diced
- 1 can (14.5 ounces) diced tomatoes
- 2 tablespoons tomato paste
- 1 teaspoon dried thyme
- 1 teaspoon dried oregano
- 1/2 cup freeze-dried vegetables (a mix of bell peppers, zucchini, and eggplant)

- For the Grilled Chicken:

- 4 boneless, skinless chicken breasts
- Salt and pepper, to taste
- 1 tablespoon olive oil

Instructions:

1) Preheat your grill to medium heat.

2) Season the chicken breasts with salt and pepper. Drizzle olive oil over the chicken to coat it.

3) Grill the chicken breasts for about 6-8 minutes per side, or until they are cooked through. Remove from heat and let them rest for a few minutes. Slice the chicken breasts into thin strips.

4) In a large skillet, heat olive oil over medium heat. Add the sliced onion and minced garlic. Sauté until the onion becomes translucent and the garlic becomes fragrant.

5) Add the diced eggplant, diced zucchini, diced yellow bell pepper, and diced red bell pepper to the skillet. Cook for about 5 minutes, or until the vegetables start to soften.

6) Stir in the diced tomatoes, tomato paste, dried thyme, dried oregano, salt, and pepper. Mix well to combine.

7) Reduce the heat to low and let the ratatouille simmer for about 30 minutes, stirring occasionally.

8) Meanwhile, place the freeze-dried vegetables in a bowl and cover them with hot water. Let them rehydrate for about 5 minutes, then drain them.

9) Stir the rehydrated freeze-dried vegetables into the ratatouille and cook for an additional 5 minutes.

10) Serve the ratatouille with grilled chicken on top. Garnish with fresh basil, if desired.

Nutrition Data:

Calories: 380 | Protein: 36g | Carbohydrates: 24g | Dietary Fiber: 9g | Sugar: 12g | Fat: 16g | Saturated Fat: 2.5g | Sodium: 460mg | Potassium: 1300mg

Seafood Paella with Freeze-Dried Mussels and Shrimp

Preparation Time: 20 minutes | Cooking Time: 45 minutes | Portion Size: 4 servings

Ingredients:

- 2 tablespoons olive oil
- 1 onion, chopped
- 2 cloves garlic, minced
- 1 red bell pepper, diced
- 1 yellow bell pepper, diced
- 1 cup Arborio rice
- 1 teaspoon smoked paprika
- 1/2 teaspoon saffron threads
- 1 can (14.5 ounces) diced tomatoes
- 2 cups vegetable broth
- 1 cup frozen peas
- 1/2 cup freeze-dried mussels
- 1/2 cup freeze-dried shrimp
- Salt and pepper, to taste
- Fresh parsley, for garnish (optional)
- Lemon wedges, for serving

Instructions:

1) Heat the olive oil in a large paella pan or skillet over medium heat. Add the chopped onion and minced garlic. Sauté until the onion becomes translucent and the garlic becomes fragrant.

2) Add the diced red bell pepper and yellow bell pepper to the pan. Cook for a few minutes until the peppers start to soften.

3) Stir in the Arborio rice, smoked paprika, and saffron threads. Toast the rice and spices for a minute, stirring constantly.

4) Pour in the diced tomatoes and vegetable broth. Stir well to combine.

5) Bring the mixture to a boil, then reduce the heat to low. Cover the pan and let the rice simmer for about 20-25 minutes, or until the rice is cooked and the liquid has been absorbed.

6) Stir in the frozen peas, freeze-dried mussels, and freeze-dried shrimp. Cook for an additional 5 minutes to warm through and rehydrate the seafood.

7) Season the paella with salt and pepper to taste.

8) Remove the pan from heat and let it rest for a few minutes.

9) Garnish the seafood paella with fresh parsley, if desired.

10) Serve the paella hot with lemon wedges on the side.

11) Enjoy your flavorful seafood paella with freeze-dried mussels and shrimp!

Nutrition Data:

Calories: 420 | Protein: 15g | Carbohydrates: 72g | Dietary Fiber: 6g | Sugar: 7g | Fat: 9g | Saturated Fat: 1g | Sodium: 800mg | Potassium: 550mg

Roasted Pork Loin with Freeze-Dried Apricot and Sage

Preparation time: 20 minutes | Cooking time: 90 minutes | Portion size: 6 servings

Ingredients:

- 2 pounds of boneless pork loin
- 1 cup freeze-dried apricots
- 1/2 cup freeze-dried sage, crushed
- 1/2 cup freeze-dried breadcrumbs
- 1/4 cup freeze-dried onions, rehydrated and chopped
- 2 cloves garlic, minced
- 1/4 cup unsalted butter, melted
- 1 teaspoon salt
- 1/2 teaspoon black pepper
- 1 cup chicken broth

Instructions:

1. Preheat the oven to 350°F (175°C).

2. In a mixing bowl, combine the rehydrated onions, minced garlic, freeze-dried apricots, freeze-dried sage, breadcrumbs, melted butter, salt, and black pepper. Mix well to form the stuffing mixture.

3. Butterfly the pork loin by making a lengthwise cut down the center of the meat, but not cutting all the way through. Open up the pork loin like a book.

4. Spread the stuffing mixture evenly over the inside of the pork loin. Roll up the loin tightly and secure it with kitchen twine at regular intervals.

5. Put the chicken broth into the bottom of a roasting pan and lay the filled pork loin on top.

6. The pork belly should be cooked for 1 hour and 30 minutes in a hot oven or until a meat thermometer reads 145°F (63°C) on the inside.

7. Take the pork belly out of the oven and let it sit for 10 minutes before slicing.

8. Slice the roasted pork loin into thick slices and serve with the pan juices.

Nutrition data:

Calories: 320 | Protein: 30g | Carbohydrates: 10g | Dietary Fiber: 2g | Sugar: 6g | Fat: 17g | Saturated Fat: 7g | Sodium: 550mg | Potassium: 600mg

Beef Bourguignon with Freeze-Dried Pearl Onions and Mushrooms

Preparation Time: 30 minutes | Cooking Time: 150 minutes | Portion Size: 6 servings

Ingredients:

- 2 pounds beef stew meat, cut into cubes
- Salt and pepper, to taste
- 2 tablespoons all-purpose flour
- 2 tablespoons olive oil
- 4 slices bacon, chopped
- 1 onion, chopped
- 3 cloves garlic, minced
- 2 carrots, sliced
- 1 cup frozen pearl onions
- 1 cup freeze-dried mushrooms
- 2 cups red wine (such as Burgundy or Pinot Noir)
- 2 cups beef broth
- 2 tablespoons tomato paste
- 1 teaspoon dried thyme
- 2 bay leaves
- Fresh parsley, for garnish (optional)

Instructions:

1) Preheat the oven to 325°F (163°C).

2) Season the beef stew meat with salt and pepper. Dredge the meat in flour, shaking off any excess.

3) Heat the olive oil in a large Dutch oven or oven-safe pot over medium-high heat. Add the bacon and cook until crispy. Remove the bacon and set it aside.

4) In the same pot, brown the beef stew meat on all sides, working in batches if necessary. Remove the meat and set it aside.

5) Add the chopped onion, minced garlic, and sliced carrots to the pot. Sauté until the vegetables become tender and fragrant.

6) Stir in the frozen pearl onions and freeze-dried mushrooms. Cook for a few minutes to rehydrate the onions and mushrooms.

7) Return the beef stew meat and bacon to the pot. Pour in the red wine and beef broth. Stir in the tomato paste, dried thyme, and bay leaves.

8) Bring the mixture to a boil, then cover the pot and transfer it to the preheated oven.

9) Bake for about 2 hours, or until the beef is tender and the flavors have melded together.

10) Remove the pot from the oven and discard the bay leaves. Adjust the seasoning with salt and pepper if needed.

11) Serve the beef bourguignon hot, garnished with fresh parsley if desired. It pairs well with mashed potatoes or crusty bread.

Nutrition Data:

Calories: 380 | Protein: 30g | Carbohydrates: 12g | Dietary Fiber: 2g | Sugar: 4g | Fat: 18g | Saturated Fat: 6g | Sodium: 600mg | Potassium: 700mg

Vegan Shepherd's Pie with Freeze-Dried Lentils and Root Vegetables

Preparation Time: 30 minutes | Cooking Time: 1 hour | Portion Size: 6 servings

Ingredients:

- For the Filling:

- 1 cup freeze-dried lentils
- 2 tablespoons olive oil
- 1 onion, chopped
- 2 cloves garlic, minced
- 2 carrots, diced
- 2 stalks celery, diced
- 1 cup frozen peas
- 1 cup vegetable broth
- 2 tablespoons tomato paste
- 1 teaspoon dried thyme
- Salt and pepper, to taste

- For the Mashed Potatoes:

- 4 large potatoes, peeled and diced
- 1/2 cup unsweetened non-dairy milk
- 2 tablespoons vegan butter
- Salt and pepper, to taste

Instructions:

1) Preheat the oven to 375°F (190°C).

2) In a bowl, rehydrate the freeze-dried lentils by pouring boiling water over them and letting them sit for about 10 minutes. Drain and set aside.

3) In a large skillet, heat the olive oil over medium heat. Add the chopped onion and minced garlic, and sauté until they become fragrant and translucent.

4) Add the diced carrots and celery to the skillet and cook for a few minutes until they begin to soften.

5) Stir in the rehydrated lentils, frozen peas, vegetable broth, tomato paste, dried thyme, salt, and pepper. Cook for another 5 minutes, allowing the flavors to combine. Remove from heat.

6) Meanwhile, place the diced potatoes in a pot and cover them with water. Bring to a boil and cook until the potatoes are tender when pierced with a fork.

7) Drain the cooked potatoes and return them to the pot. Add the non-dairy milk and vegan butter. Mash the potatoes until smooth and creamy. Season with salt and pepper to taste.

8) Transfer the lentil and vegetable filling to a baking dish. Spread the mashed potatoes evenly over the filling.

9) Bake in the preheated oven for about 30 minutes, or until the top is golden and the filling is bubbling.

10) Remove from the oven and let it cool for a few minutes before serving.

Nutrition Data:

Calories: 300 | Protein: 10g | Carbohydrates: 50g | Dietary Fiber: 10g | Sugar: 6g | Fat: 8g | Saturated Fat: 2g | Sodium: 400mg | Potassium: 1200mg

Spaghetti Marinara with Freeze-Dried Shrimp and Basil

Preparation Time: 10 minutes | Cooking Time: 25 minutes | Portion Size: 4 servings

Ingredients:

- 8 ounces spaghetti
- 2 tablespoons olive oil
- 3 cloves garlic, minced
- 1 can (14 ounces) crushed tomatoes
- 1/2 teaspoon dried oregano
- Salt and pepper, to taste
- 1/2 cup freeze-dried shrimp
- 1/4 cup chopped fresh basil
- Grated Parmesan cheese, for serving (optional)

Instructions:

1) Cook the spaghetti according to the package instructions until al dente. Drain and set aside.

2) In a large skillet, heat the olive oil over medium heat. Add the minced garlic and sauté for 1 minute until fragrant.

3) Stir in the crushed tomatoes, dried oregano, salt, and pepper. Simmer the marinara sauce for about 10 minutes to allow the flavors to meld together.

4) While the sauce is simmering, rehydrate the freeze-dried shrimp by placing them in a bowl and pouring boiling water over them. Let them sit for 5 minutes, then drain.

5) Add the rehydrated shrimp to the marinara sauce and cook for an additional 2-3 minutes, until the shrimp is heated through.

6) Toss the cooked spaghetti in the sauce until well coated.

7) Remove the skillet from the heat and stir in the chopped fresh basil.

8) Serve the spaghetti marinara hot, optionally garnished with grated Parmesan cheese.

Nutrition Data:

Calories: 350 | Protein: 12g | Carbohydrates: 55g | Dietary Fiber: 4g | Sugar: 6g | Fat: 10g | Saturated Fat: 2g | Sodium: 500mg | Potassium: 400mg

Chicken Tagine with Freeze-Dried Apricots & Chickpeas

Preparation Time: 15 minutes | Cooking Time: 150 minutes | Portion Size: 4 servings

Ingredients:

- 4 chicken thighs, bone-in and skin-on
- 2 tablespoons olive oil
- 1 onion, chopped
- 2 cloves garlic, minced
- 1 teaspoon ground cumin
- 1 teaspoon ground coriander
- 1/2 teaspoon ground cinnamon
- 1/2 teaspoon ground turmeric
- 1/4 teaspoon ground ginger
- 1/4 teaspoon cayenne pepper (optional, for heat)
- Salt and pepper, to taste
- 1 cup freeze-dried apricots
- 1 can (14 ounces) diced tomatoes
- 1 can (14 ounces) chickpeas, drained and rinsed
- 1 cup vegetable broth
- Chopped fresh cilantro, for garnish

Instructions:

1)   In a large, deep skillet or tagine, heat the olive oil over medium heat. Season the chicken thighs with salt and pepper, then brown them on both sides in the hot oil. Remove the chicken from the skillet and set aside.

2)   In the same skillet, add the chopped onion and minced garlic. Sauté until the onion becomes translucent and fragrant.

3)   Add the ground cumin, ground coriander, ground cinnamon, ground turmeric, ground ginger, cayenne pepper (if using), salt, and pepper to the skillet. Stir well to coat the onions and garlic with the spices.

4)   Return the browned chicken thighs to the skillet and add the freeze-dried apricots, diced tomatoes, chickpeas, and vegetable broth. Stir to combine all the ingredients.

5)   Cover the skillet and simmer the tagine over low heat for about 1 hour, or until the chicken is cooked through and tender.

6)   Taste and adjust the seasoning if needed.

7)   Serve the Moroccan chicken tagine hot, garnished with chopped fresh cilantro. Accompany with couscous or rice, if desired.

Nutrition Data:

Calories: 350 | Protein: 25g | Carbohydrates: 30g | Dietary Fiber: 7g | Sugar: 16g | Fat: 15g | Saturated Fat: 3g | Sodium: 600mg | Potassium: 700mg

Grilled Steak with Freeze-Dried Chimichurri Sauce

Preparation Time: 10 minutes | Cooking Time: 10 minutes | Portion Size: 2 servings

Ingredients:

- 2 beef steaks (such as ribeye, sirloin, or striploin), about 8 ounces each
- Salt and pepper, to taste
- 1 tablespoon olive oil
- 1 tablespoon red wine vinegar
- 1 tablespoon freeze-dried parsley
- 1 tablespoon freeze-dried cilantro
- 1 tablespoon freeze-dried oregano
- 2 cloves garlic, minced
- 1/2 teaspoon red pepper flakes (optional, for heat)

Instructions:

1) Preheat your grill to medium-high heat.

2) Season the steaks with salt and pepper on both sides.

3) In a small bowl, combine the olive oil, red wine vinegar, freeze-dried parsley, freeze-dried cilantro, freeze-dried oregano, minced garlic, and red pepper flakes (if using). Stir well to make the chimichurri sauce.

4) Place the steaks on the preheated grill and cook for about 4-5 minutes per side for medium-rare, or adjust the cooking time according to your preferred doneness.

5) Remove the steaks from the grill and let them rest for a few minutes.

6) Drizzle the chimichurri sauce over the grilled steaks or serve it on the side as a dipping sauce.

7) Enjoy the grilled steak with the flavorful freeze-dried chimichurri sauce.

Nutrition Data:

Calories: 400 | Protein: 40g | Carbohydrates: 1g | Dietary Fiber: 0g | Sugar: 0g | Fat: 26g | Saturated Fat: 9g | Sodium: 80mg | Potassium: 600mg

Vegan Soba Noodle Soup with Freeze-Dried Tofu and Vegetables

Preparation Time: 10 minutes | Cooking Time: 20 minutes | Portion Size: 4 servings

Ingredients:

- 8 ounces soba noodles
- 1 tablespoon sesame oil
- 1 small onion, thinly sliced
- 2 cloves garlic, minced
- 1 tablespoon grated ginger
- 4 cups vegetable broth
- 2 cups water
- 1 cup freeze-dried tofu, rehydrated and sliced
- 1 cup freeze-dried mixed vegetables, rehydrated
- 2 tablespoons soy sauce
- 1 tablespoon rice vinegar
- 1 tablespoon miso paste
- 1 teaspoon sriracha sauce (optional, for heat)
- 2 green onions, thinly sliced
- Sesame seeds, for garnish

Instructions:

1) Cook the soba noodles according to the package instructions. Drain and set aside.

2) In a large pot, heat the sesame oil over medium heat. Add the sliced onion, minced garlic, and grated ginger. Sauté until the onion is translucent and fragrant.

3) Add the vegetable broth and water to the pot. Bring to a boil and then reduce heat to a simmer.

4) Stir in the rehydrated freeze-dried tofu and mixed vegetables. Cook for about 5 minutes until the vegetables are tender.

5) In a small bowl, whisk together the soy sauce, rice vinegar, miso paste, and sriracha sauce (if using). Add the mixture to the soup and stir well to combine.

6) Divide the cooked soba noodles among serving bowls. Ladle the hot soup over the noodles.

7) Garnish with sliced green onions and sprinkle with sesame seeds.

8) Serve the vegan soba noodle soup immediately.

Nutrition Data:

Calories: 250 | Protein: 10g | Carbohydrates: 40g | Dietary Fiber: 6g | Sugar: 4g | Fat: 5g | Saturated Fat: 1g | Sodium: 800mg | Potassium: 400mg

Bouillabaisse with Freeze-Dried Seafood and Fennel

Preparation Time: 30 minutes | Cooking Time: 40 minutes | Portion Size: 4 servings

Ingredients:

- 2 tablespoons olive oil
- 1 onion, chopped
- 2 cloves garlic, minced
- 1 fennel bulb, thinly sliced
- 1 carrot, sliced
- 1 celery stalk, sliced
- 1 teaspoon dried thyme
- 1 teaspoon dried oregano
- 1 bay leaf
- 1 can (14 oz) diced tomatoes
- 4 cups vegetable broth
- 1 cup white wine
- 1 cup water
- 1 cup freeze-dried seafood medley (shrimp, mussels, calamari), rehydrated
- Salt and pepper to taste
- Fresh parsley, chopped, for garnish
- Crusty bread, for serving

Instructions:

1) In a large pot, heat the olive oil over medium heat. Add the chopped onion and minced garlic. Sauté until the onion becomes translucent.

2) Add the sliced fennel, carrot, and celery to the pot. Cook for about 5 minutes until the vegetables start to soften.

3) Stir in the dried thyme, dried oregano, and bay leaf. Cook for an additional 1-2 minutes to release the fragrance of the herbs.

4) Add the diced tomatoes, vegetable broth, white wine, and water to the pot. Bring to a boil and then reduce heat to a simmer. Let the soup simmer for about 20 minutes to allow the flavors to meld together.

5) Stir in the rehydrated freeze-dried seafood medley. Continue to simmer for another 10 minutes until the seafood is cooked through.

6) Season the bouillabaisse with salt and pepper to taste.

7) Ladle the soup into bowls and garnish with freshly chopped parsley.

8) Serve the bouillabaisse with crusty bread on the side.

Nutrition Data:

Calories: 250 | Protein: 15g | Carbohydrates: 15g | Dietary Fiber: 4g | Sugar: 6g | Fat: 10g | Saturated Fat: 2g | Sodium: 800mg | Potassium: 500mg

Roast Duck with Freeze-Dried Plum Sauce and Bok Choy

Preparation Time: 30 minutes | Cooking Time: 2 hours | Portion Size: 4 servings

Ingredients:

- 1 whole duck (about 4-5 lbs)
- Salt and pepper to taste
- 1 tablespoon Chinese five-spice powder
- 2 tablespoons vegetable oil
- 1 cup freeze-dried plum sauce, rehydrated
- 2 tablespoons soy sauce
- 2 tablespoons rice vinegar
- 2 tablespoons honey
- 4 baby bok choy, halved lengthwise

Instructions:

1) Preheat the oven to 350°F (175°C).

2) Rinse the duck under cold water and pat it dry with paper towels. Season the duck with salt, pepper, and Chinese five-spice powder, rubbing the spices into the skin.

3) Heat a large oven-safe skillet or roasting pan over medium-high heat. Add the vegetable oil and heat until shimmering. Place the duck in the skillet, breast side down, and sear for about 5 minutes until the skin is browned and crispy. Flip the duck and sear the other side for an additional 5 minutes.

4) Transfer the skillet or roasting pan with the duck to the preheated oven. Roast for about 1.5 to 2 hours, or until the internal temperature of the duck reaches 165°F (74°C) when measured with a meat thermometer inserted into the thickest part of the thigh.

5) While the duck is roasting, prepare the plum sauce. In a small saucepan, combine the rehydrated freeze-dried plum sauce, soy sauce, rice vinegar, and honey. Heat the sauce over low heat, stirring occasionally, until warmed through.

6) About 20 minutes before the duck is done, place the halved bok choy around the duck in the skillet or roasting pan. Drizzle the bok choy with a little oil and season with salt and pepper. Return the skillet or roasting pan to the oven and continue roasting until the bok choy is tender-crisp.

7) Remove the duck from the oven and let it rest for 10 minutes before carving. Slice the duck into serving pieces.

8) Serve the roast duck with the plum sauce and the roasted bok choy.

Nutrition Data:

Calories: 450 | Protein: 35g | Carbohydrates: 10g | Dietary Fiber: 2g | Sugar: 8g | Fat: 30g | Saturated Fat: 8g | Sodium: 800mg | Potassium: 600mg

Lamb Curry with Freeze-Dried Peas and Potatoes

Preparation Time: 20 minutes | Cooking Time: 2 hours | Portion Size: 4 servings

Ingredients:

- 1.5 lbs boneless lamb, cut into cubes
- 2 tablespoons vegetable oil
- 1 large onion, finely chopped
- 3 cloves garlic, minced
- 1 tablespoon ginger, grated
- 2 tablespoons curry powder
- 1 teaspoon ground cumin
- 1 teaspoon ground coriander
- 1/2 teaspoon turmeric
- 1/4 teaspoon cayenne pepper (optional, for heat)
- 1 cup diced tomatoes
- 2 cups water
- 1 cup freeze-dried peas, rehydrated
- 2 medium potatoes, peeled and diced
- Fresh cilantro, chopped (for garnish)

Instructions:

1) Heat the vegetable oil in a large pot or Dutch oven over medium heat. Add the chopped onion and cook until it becomes soft and translucent, about 5 minutes.

2) Add the minced garlic and grated ginger to the pot and cook for another minute until fragrant.

3) Add the lamb cubes to the pot and cook until they are browned on all sides. This will take about 5-7 minutes.

4) In a small bowl, combine the curry powder, ground cumin, ground coriander, turmeric, and cayenne pepper (if using). Mix well.

5) Sprinkle the spice mixture over the browned lamb cubes and stir to coat the meat evenly. Cook for an additional 2 minutes to toast the spices.

6) Add the diced tomatoes to the pot and stir to combine with the lamb and spices. Cook for 2-3 minutes, allowing the tomatoes to break down and release their juices.

7) Pour in the water and bring the mixture to a boil. Reduce the heat to low, cover the pot, and let it simmer for about 1.5 hours, or until the lamb is tender.

8) Add the rehydrated freeze-dried peas and diced potatoes to the pot. Stir well to incorporate them into the curry. Cover the pot again and continue to simmer for another 20-30 minutes, or until the potatoes are cooked through.

9) Season the curry with salt and pepper to taste. Adjust the spice level by adding more cayenne pepper if desired. Serve the lamb with cilnantro. It pairs well with rice or naan bread.

Nutrition Data:

Calories: 450 | Protein: 30g | Carbohydrates: 30g | Dietary Fiber: 6g | Sugar: 5g | Fat: 25g | Saturated Fat: 10g | Sodium: 600mg | Potassium: 900mg

Vegan Stuffed Bell Peppers with Freeze-Dried Quinoa and Black Beans

Preparation Time: 20 minutes | Cooking Time: 40 minutes | Portion Size: 4 servings

Ingredients:

- 4 large bell peppers (any color)
- 1 cup freeze-dried quinoa
- 1 can black beans, drained and rinsed
- 1 cup corn kernels (fresh or frozen)
- 1 small onion, finely chopped
- 2 cloves garlic, minced
- 1 teaspoon cumin
- 1/2 teaspoon paprika
- 1/2 teaspoon chili powder
- Salt and pepper to taste
- 1 cup tomato sauce
- Fresh cilantro, chopped (for garnish)

Instructions:

1) Preheat the oven to 375°F (190°C).

2) Cut off the tops of the bell peppers and remove the seeds and membranes from the inside. Rinse the peppers under cold water and set them aside.

3) In a bowl, rehydrate the freeze-dried quinoa according to the package instructions. Once rehydrated, drain any excess liquid.

4) In a large skillet, heat some oil over medium heat. Add the chopped onion and minced garlic and sauté until the onion becomes translucent.

5) Add the cooked quinoa, black beans, corn kernels, cumin, paprika, chili powder, salt, and pepper to the skillet. Stir well to combine all the ingredients and cook for an additional 2-3 minutes to let the flavors meld.

6) Pour the tomato sauce into the skillet and stir until everything is coated evenly. Cook for another 2-3 minutes, then remove the skillet from the heat.

7) Stuff each bell pepper with the quinoa and black bean mixture, pressing it down gently to fill the peppers completely.

8) Place the stuffed peppers in a baking dish and cover the dish with aluminum foil. Bake in the preheated oven for 30 minutes.

9) Remove the foil and bake for an additional 10 minutes, or until the peppers are tender and slightly browned.

10) Once cooked, remove the stuffed peppers from the oven and let them cool for a few minutes. Garnish with freshly chopped cilantro before serving.

Nutrition Data:

Calories: 280 | Protein: 12g | Carbohydrates: 56g | Dietary Fiber: 12g | Sugar: 7g | Fat: 2g | Saturated Fat: 0g | Sodium: 600mg | Potassium: 900mg

Lobster Thermidor with Freeze-Dried Mushrooms

Preparation Time: 30 minutes | Cooking Time: 30 minutes | Portion Size: 4 servings

Ingredients:

- 2 lobster tails
- 1/2 cup freeze-dried mushrooms
- 2 tablespoons butter
- 2 tablespoons all-purpose flour
- 1 cup milk
- 1/2 cup grated Parmesan cheese
- 2 tablespoons Dijon mustard
- 2 tablespoons fresh parsley, chopped
- Salt and pepper to taste
- Lemon wedges (for serving)

Instructions:

1) Preheat the oven to 400°F (200°C).

2) In a bowl, rehydrate the freeze-dried mushrooms according to the package instructions. Once rehydrated, drain any excess liquid and set aside.

3) Bring a pot of water to a boil. Add the lobster tails and cook for about 5-7 minutes, until the shells turn bright red and the meat is opaque. Remove the lobster tails from the water and let them cool slightly.

4) Once the lobster tails are cool enough to handle, use kitchen shears to carefully cut through the top of the shells lengthwise. Gently remove the meat from the shells and chop it into bite-sized pieces. Set aside.

5) In a saucepan, melt the butter over medium heat. Add the rehydrated mushrooms and sauté for 2-3 minutes until they are slightly softened.

6) Sprinkle the flour over the mushrooms and stir well to coat them evenly. Cook for an additional 1-2 minutes, stirring constantly.

7) Gradually pour in the milk while whisking continuously to prevent lumps from forming. Cook the mixture until it thickens and comes to a simmer.

8) Remove the saucepan from the heat and stir in the grated Parmesan cheese, Dijon mustard, and chopped parsley. Season with salt and pepper to taste.

9) Add the chopped lobster meat to the sauce and mix gently to combine.

10) Spoon the lobster mixture back into the lobster shells, dividing it evenly.

11) Place the stuffed lobster tails on a baking sheet and bake in the preheated oven for about 10-15 minutes, until the tops are golden brown and bubbling.

12) Remove from the oven and let the lobster thermidor cool for a few minutes before serving. Serve with lemon wedges on the side.

Nutrition Data:

Calories: 340 | Protein: 28g | Carbohydrates: 9g | Dietary Fiber: 1g | Sugar: 4g | Fat: 20g | Saturated Fat: 12g | Sodium: 590mg | Potassium: 410mg

Chicken Marsala with Freeze-Dried Mushrooms

Preparation Time: 15 minutes | Cooking Time: 30 minutes | Portion Size: 4 servings

Ingredients:

- 4 chicken breasts, boneless and skinless
- 1/2 cup all-purpose flour
- Salt and pepper to taste
- 2 tablespoons olive oil
- 4 tablespoons butter
- 1/2 cup freeze-dried mushrooms
- 2 shallots, thinly sliced
- 1 cup Marsala wine
- 1 cup chicken broth
- 1/2 cup heavy cream
- Fresh parsley, chopped (for garnish)

Instructions:

1)   In a shallow dish, combine the all-purpose flour, salt, and pepper. Dredge the chicken breasts in the flour mixture, shaking off any excess.

2)   Heat the olive oil and 2 tablespoons of butter in a large skillet over medium-high heat. Add the chicken breasts and cook for about 4-5 minutes per side, or until golden brown and cooked through. Remove the chicken from the skillet and set aside.

3)   In the same skillet, melt the remaining 2 tablespoons of butter. Add the freeze-dried mushrooms and shallots, and sauté until the shallots are translucent and the mushrooms are slightly softened.

4)   Pour in the Marsala wine and bring it to a simmer, scraping the bottom of the skillet to release any browned bits. Allow the wine to reduce by half.

5)   Stir in the chicken broth and bring the mixture to a boil. Reduce the heat to low and simmer for about 5 minutes, allowing the flavors to blend together.

6)   Stir in the heavy cream and simmer for an additional 2-3 minutes, until the sauce thickens slightly. Season with salt and pepper to taste.

7)   Return the cooked chicken breasts to the skillet, nestling them into the sauce. Cook for a few more minutes to heat the chicken through.

8)   Garnish with fresh chopped parsley and serve the chicken Marsala hot with your choice of side dishes.

Nutrition Data:

Calories: 380 | Protein: 32g | Carbohydrates: 12g | Dietary Fiber: 1g | Sugar: 3g | Fat: 18g | Saturated Fat: 9g | Sodium: 420mg | Potassium: 580mg

Beef and Broccoli Stir-Fry with Freeze-Dried Peppers and Sesame Seeds

Preparation Time: 15 minutes | Cooking Time: 15 minutes | Portion Size: 4 servings

Ingredients:

- 1 lb beef sirloin, thinly sliced
- 3 tablespoons soy sauce
- 2 tablespoons oyster sauce
- 1 tablespoon cornstarch
- 2 tablespoons vegetable oil
- 4 cloves garlic, minced
- 1 teaspoon ginger, grated
- 1 cup freeze-dried bell peppers
- 2 cups broccoli florets
- 1/2 cup beef broth
- 1 tablespoon sesame oil
- 1 tablespoon sesame seeds, toasted

Instructions:

1) In a bowl, combine the soy sauce, oyster sauce, and cornstarch. Add the sliced beef to the bowl and toss to coat. Let it marinate for 10 minutes.

2) Heat the vegetable oil in a large skillet or wok over high heat. Add the minced garlic and grated ginger, and sauté for about 30 seconds until fragrant.

3) Add the marinated beef to the skillet and stir-fry for 2-3 minutes until browned. Remove the beef from the skillet and set aside.

4) In the same skillet, add the freeze-dried bell peppers and broccoli florets. Stir-fry for 3-4 minutes until the vegetables are tender-crisp.

5) Pour in the beef broth and bring it to a simmer. Cook for another 2 minutes to allow the flavors to blend.

6) Return the cooked beef to the skillet and stir-fry for an additional 1-2 minutes to heat through.

7) Drizzle the sesame oil over the stir-fry and toss to coat evenly.

8) Sprinkle the toasted sesame seeds on top for added flavor and crunch.

9) Serve the beef and broccoli stir-fry hot over steamed rice or noodles.

Nutrition Data:

Calories: 320 | Protein: 26g | Carbohydrates: 12g | Dietary Fiber: 3g | Sugar: 4g | Fat: 18g | Saturated Fat: 3g | Sodium: 840mg | Potassium: 650mg

Vegan Thai Green Curry with Freeze-Dried Bamboo Shoots and Eggplant

Preparation Time: 15 minutes | Cooking Time: 20 minutes | Portion Size: 4 servings

Ingredients:

- 1 tablespoon vegetable oil
- 1 onion, sliced
- 2 garlic cloves, minced
- 2 tablespoons green curry paste
- 1 can (14 oz) coconut milk
- 1 cup vegetable broth
- 1 cup freeze-dried bamboo shoots
- 1 small eggplant, cut into cubes
- 1 red bell pepper, sliced
- 1 cup frozen green peas
- 1 tablespoon soy sauce
- 1 tablespoon lime juice
- 2 tablespoons fresh basil leaves, chopped
- Cooked rice, for serving

Instructions:

1) Heat the vegetable oil in a large pan over medium heat. Add the sliced onion and minced garlic, and sauté for 2-3 minutes until the onion becomes translucent.

2) Add the green curry paste to the pan and cook for another minute, stirring continuously.

3) Pour in the coconut milk and vegetable broth. Stir well to combine the curry paste with the liquids.

4) Add the freeze-dried bamboo shoots, eggplant cubes, and sliced red bell pepper to the pan. Stir to coat the vegetables with the curry sauce.

5) Bring the mixture to a simmer and let it cook for about 10 minutes, or until the vegetables are tender.

6) Add the frozen green peas and stir them into the curry. Cook for an additional 2-3 minutes until the peas are heated through.

7) Stir in the soy sauce and lime juice. Taste and adjust the seasonings if needed.

8) Remove the pan from the heat and sprinkle the chopped fresh basil leaves over the curry. Stir gently to incorporate the basil.

9) Serve the vegan Thai green curry hot over cooked rice.

Nutrition Data:

Calories: 280 | Protein: 5g | Carbohydrates: 19g | Dietary Fiber: 6g | Sugar: 7g | Fat: 21g | Saturated Fat: 16g | Sodium: 600mg | Potassium: 520mg

Seafood Linguine with Freeze-Dried Clams and Parsley

Preparation Time: 10 minutes | Cooking Time: 20 minutes | Portion Size: 4 servings

Ingredients:

- 8 ounces linguine pasta
- 2 tablespoons olive oil
- 2 garlic cloves, minced
- 1/2 teaspoon red pepper flakes (optional)
- 1/2 cup white wine
- 1 cup vegetable broth
- 1 cup freeze-dried clams
- 8 ounces shrimp, peeled and deveined
- 8 ounces scallops
- 1/4 cup chopped fresh parsley
- Salt and pepper, to taste
- Lemon wedges, for serving

Instructions:

1) Cook the linguine pasta according to the package instructions until al dente. Drain and set aside.

2) In a large skillet, heat the olive oil over medium heat. Add the minced garlic and red pepper flakes (if using) and sauté for about 1 minute until fragrant.

3) Pour in the white wine and let it simmer for 2 minutes to reduce slightly.

4) Add the vegetable broth and freeze-dried clams to the skillet. Stir well and bring to a simmer.

5) Add the shrimp and scallops to the skillet. Cook for about 4-5 minutes until the seafood is cooked through and opaque.

6) Stir in the cooked linguine pasta and toss to coat it with the sauce.

7) Add the chopped parsley and season with salt and pepper to taste. Give it a final toss to incorporate all the ingredients.

8) Remove from heat and serve the seafood linguine with lemon wedges on the side.

Nutrition Data:

Calories: 380 | Protein: 25g | Carbohydrates: 40g | Dietary Fiber: 3g | Sugar: 2g | Fat: 10g | Saturated Fat: 1.5g | Sodium: 380mg | Potassium: 480mg

Chicken & Sausage Gumbo with Freeze-Dried Okra

Preparation Time: 20 minutes | Cooking Time: 90 minutes | Portion Size: 6 servings

Ingredients:

- 1/4 cup vegetable oil
- 1/4 cup all-purpose flour
- 1 large onion, diced
- 1 green bell pepper, diced
- 2 celery stalks, diced
- 3 cloves garlic, minced
- 1 pound boneless, skinless chicken thighs, cut into bite-sized pieces
- 8 ounces smoked sausage, sliced
- 1 teaspoon paprika
- 1 teaspoon dried thyme
- 1 teaspoon dried oregano
- 1/2 teaspoon cayenne pepper (adjust to taste)
- 1/2 teaspoon salt (adjust to taste)
- 1/4 teaspoon black pepper
- 4 cups chicken broth
- 1 cup freeze-dried okra
- 1 can (14.5 ounces) diced tomatoes
- 2 bay leaves
- Cooked white rice, for serving
- Chopped green onions, for garnish

Instructions:

1) In a large pot or Dutch oven, heat the vegetable oil over medium heat. Add the flour and stir continuously to make a roux. Cook the roux, stirring constantly, until it turns a dark brown color, about 20 minutes. Be careful not to burn it.

2) Add the diced onion, bell pepper, celery, and minced garlic to the pot. Cook for 5 minutes, stirring occasionally, until the vegetables have softened.

3) Add the chicken thighs and smoked sausage to the pot. Cook for about 5 minutes, until the chicken is lightly browned.

4) Stir in the paprika, dried thyme, dried oregano, cayenne pepper, salt, and black pep-per. Mix well to coat the meat and vegetables with the spices.

5) Pour in the chicken broth and bring the mixture to a boil. Reduce the heat to low and let it simmer, uncovered, for 30 minutes.

6) Add the freeze-dried okra, diced toma-toes (with their juice), and bay leaves to the pot. Stir well and simmer for another 30 min-utes.

7) Remove the bay leaves and taste the gum-bo. Adjust the seasoning with salt and cay-enne pepper if needed.

8) Serve the Cajun Chicken and Sausage Gumbo over cooked white rice. Garnish with chopped green onions.

Nutrition Data:

Calories: 380 | Protein: 22g | Carbohydrates: 20g | Dietary Fiber: 4g | Sugar: 5g | Fat: 25g | Saturated Fat: 6g | Sodium: 900mg | Potassium: 590mg

Lentil and Vegetable Curry with Freeze-Dried Spinach and Cauliflower

Preparation Time: 15 minutes | Cooking Time: 40 minutes | Portion Size: 4 servings

Ingredients:

- 1 tablespoon vegetable oil
- 1 onion, diced
- 2 cloves garlic, minced
- 1 tablespoon curry powder
- 1 teaspoon ground cumin
- 1/2 teaspoon ground turmeric
- 1/4 teaspoon cayenne pepper (adjust to taste)
- 1 cup dry lentils
- 3 cups vegetable broth
- 1 can (14.5 ounces) diced tomatoes
- 1 cup freeze-dried spinach
- 2 cups cauliflower florets
- 1 can (13.5 ounces) coconut milk
- Salt, to taste
- Chopped fresh cilantro, for garnish
- Cooked rice or naan bread, for serving

Instructions:

1) Heat the vegetable oil in a large pot or Dutch oven over medium heat. Add the diced onion and cook until it becomes translucent, about 5 minutes. Stir in the minced garlic and cook for an additional 1 minute.

2) Add the curry powder, ground cumin, ground turmeric, and cayenne pepper to the pot. Stir well to coat the onions and garlic with the spices. Cook for 1 minute to release their flavors.

3) Add the dry lentils to the pot and pour in the vegetable broth. Stir in the diced tomatoes, including their juice. Bring the mixture to a boil.

4) Reduce the heat to low and cover the pot. Let the lentils simmer for about 20 minutes, or until they become tender.

5) Add the freeze-dried spinach and cauliflower florets to the pot. Stir well and cook for an additional 10 minutes, until the vegetables are cooked through.

6) Pour in the coconut milk and stir to combine. Simmer the curry for another 5 minutes to allow the flavors to meld together. Season with salt to taste.

7) Remove the pot from the heat. Serve the Lentil and Vegetable Curry over cooked rice or with naan bread. Garnish with chopped fresh cilantro.

Nutrition Data:

Calories: 320 | Protein: 15g | Carbohydrates: 42g | Dietary Fiber: 14g | Sugar: 5g | Fat: 12g | Saturated Fat: 9g | Sodium: 900mg | Potassium: 900mg

Dessert

Freeze-Dried Strawberry and Banana Parfait

Preparation Time: 10 minutes | Portion Size: 2 servings

Ingredients:

- 1 cup freeze-dried strawberries
- 1 banana, sliced
- 1 cup Greek yogurt
- 2 tablespoons honey
- 1/4 cup granola

Instructions:

1) In a bowl, combine the freeze-dried strawberries and banana slices.

2) In a fresh bowl, mix the Greek yogurt and honey until well combined.

3) Take two serving glasses or jars and layer the ingredients. Start with a layer of the freeze-dried strawberry and banana mixture, followed by a layer of Greek yogurt and a sprinkle of granola. Repeat the layers until all the ingredients are used.

4) Add a final dollop of Greek yogurt and some granola to the top of the parfait before serving.

5) Serve immediately and enjoy!

Nutrition Data:

Calories: 250 | Protein: 12g | Carbohydrates: 48g | Dietary Fiber: 6g | Sugar: 28g | Fat: 3g | Saturated Fat: 0.5g | Sodium: 60mg | Potassium: 650mg

Chocolate Mousse with Freeze-Dried Raspberries

Preparation Time: 15 minutes | Portion Size: 4 servings

Ingredients:

- 4 ounces dark chocolate, chopped
- 1 cup heavy cream
- 2 tablespoons powdered sugar
- 1 teaspoon vanilla extract
- 1/4 cup freeze-dried raspberries

Instructions:

1) Start with melting the dark chocolate in a heatproof bowl placed over a pot of hot water to keep warm. Stir occasionally until smooth. Remove from heat and let it cool for a few minutes.

2) Heavy cream, powdered sugar, and vanilla extract should be whipped separately until soft peaks form.

3) Combine the melted chocolate and whipped cream by gently folding the two together.

4) Divide the chocolate mousse mixture into serving glasses or bowls.

5) Crush the freeze-dried raspberries into small pieces and sprinkle them over the top of each chocolate mousse serving.

6) Refrigerate for at least 2 hours or until the mousse is set.

7) Serve chilled, and enjoy!

Nutrition Data:

Calories: 290 | Protein: 3g | Carbohydrates: 23g | Dietary Fiber: 3g | Sugar: 16g | Fat: 23g | Saturated Fat: 14g | Sodium: 30mg | Potassium: 240mg

Vanilla and Freeze-Dried Berry Chia Pudding

Preparation Time: 10 minutes | Portion Size: 2 servings

Ingredients:

- 1/4 cup chia seeds
- 1 cup almond milk
- 1 tablespoon maple syrup or honey
- 1/2 teaspoon vanilla extract
- 1/4 cup freeze-dried mixed berries

Instructions:

1) In a mixing bowl, combine the chia seeds, almond milk, maple syrup or honey, and vanilla extract. Stir well to ensure the chia seeds are fully immersed in the liquid.

2) Let the mixture sit for about 5 minutes, then stir again to prevent clumping. Cover the bowl and refrigerate for at least 2 hours, or overnight, to allow the chia seeds to absorb the liquid and thicken.

3) Once the chia pudding has thickened to your desired consistency, give it a good stir to break up any lumps.

4) Crush the freeze-dried mixed berries into smaller pieces. You can do this by placing them in a sealed plastic bag and gently crushing them with a rolling pin or the back of a spoon.

5) Divide the chia pudding into serving glasses or bowls. Sprinkle the crushed freeze-dried berries on top of each portion.

6) Serve chilled, and enjoy!

Nutrition Data:

Calories: 150 | Protein: 4g | Carbohydrates: 19g | Dietary Fiber: 10g | Sugar: 5g | Fat: 6g | Saturated Fat: 1g | Sodium: 80mg | Potassium: 180mg

Freeze-Dried Peach and Almond Tart

Preparation Time: 20 minutes | Cooking Time: 30 minutes | Portion Size: 8 servings

Ingredients:

- For the crust:

- 1 1/2 cups all-purpose flour
- 1/4 cup granulated sugar
- 1/2 cup unsalted butter, cold in cubed
- 1 large egg yolk
- 2 tablespoons ice water

- For the filling:

- 2 cups freeze-dried peaches
- 1/4 cup almond meal
- 1/4 cup granulated sugar
- 1 tablespoon cornstarch
- 1/2 teaspoon vanilla extract
- 1/4 teaspoon almond extract
- For the topping:
- 1/4 cup sliced almonds
- 1 tablespoon powdered sugar (for dusting)

Instructions:

1. The oven needs to be preheated to 350F (175C). Lubricate a tart pan with a 9-inch diameter and a detachable bottom.

2. Place in the processor sugar and flour, and pulse until combined. Mix the dry ingredients in a food processor until they resemble coarse crumbs, and then stir in the cold, cubed butter.

3) Mix the egg yolk and ice water in a small bowl. Put the ingredients in a food processor and whir until a dough forms.

4) Transfer the dough to a floured surface and shape it into a disk. Refrigerate it in a plastic bag for 30 minutes.

5) Meanwhile, place the freeze-dried peaches in a resealable bag and crush them into smaller pieces using a rolling pin or the back of a spoon.

6) In a bowl, combine the crushed freeze-dried peaches, almond meal, granulated sugar, cornstarch, vanilla extract, and almond extract. Mix well.

7) The dough should be chilled before being rolled out on a floured surface into a circle that is just slightly bigger than the tart pan. Trim any excess dough and gently push it into the prepared pan.

8) Spread the peach filling evenly over the tart crust. Sprinkle the sliced almonds on top.

9) If you want a golden crust and a firm filling, bake the tart pan in a preheated oven for 25 to 30 minutes.

10) Take the tart out of the oven and cool it on a rack until it is room temperature. Sprinkle powdered sugar over the top once it has cooled.

Nutrition Data:

Calories: 280 | Protein: 4g | Carbohydrates: 36g | Dietary Fiber: 2g | Sugar: 15g | Fat: 13g | Saturated Fat: 7g | Sodium: 10mg | Potassium: 160mg

Freeze-Dried Mango and Coconut Sorbet

Preparation Time: 10 minutes | Cooking Time: 0 minutes | Portion Size: 4 servings

Ingredients:

- 2 cups freeze-dried mango
- 1 can (13.5 oz) coconut milk, chilled
- 1/4 cup agave syrup or honey
- 1 tablespoon lime juice
- 1/2 teaspoon vanilla extract
- Pinch of salt

Instructions:

1) Place the freeze-dried mango in a food processor or blender. Pulse until it becomes a fine powder.

2) In a large bowl, combine the mango powder, chilled coconut milk, agave syrup or honey, lime juice, vanilla extract, and salt. Make sure all the ingredients are mixed in by stirring them thoroughly.

3) Combine all ingredients and churn in an ice cream machine per the manufacturer's instructions. The sorbet needs to thicken up and turn creamy.

4) When the sorbet has the right consistency, place it in a sealed container and place it in the freezer for at least two hours to harden.

5) Before serving, allow the sorbet to soften slightly at room temperature for a few minutes. Scoop into bowls or cones and enjoy!

Nutrition Data:

Calories: 210 | Protein: 2g | Carbohydrates: 33g | Dietary Fiber: 4g | Sugar: 25g | Fat: 8g | Saturated Fat: 7g | Sodium: 30mg | Potassium: 460mg

Ricotta Cheesecake with Freeze-Dried Blueberry

Preparation Time: 20 minutes | Cooking Time: 1 hour | Portion Size: 8 servings

Ingredients:

- For the crust

- 1 1/2 cups graham cracker crumbs
- 1/4 cup melted butter
- 2 tablespoons granulated sugar

- For the filling

- 2 cups ricotta cheese
- 1 cup cream cheese
- 3/4 cup granulated sugar
- 3 large eggs
- 1 tablespoon lemon juice
- 1 teaspoon vanilla extract

- For the blueberry compote

- 1 cup freeze-dried blueberries
- 1/4 cup water
- 2 tablespoons granulated sugar
- 1 teaspoon lemon juice

Instructions:

1) Preheat the oven to 325°F (160°C). Grease a 9-inch springform pan.

2) Graham cracker crumbs, melted butter, and granulated sugar should be mixed together in a medium basin. To make the crust, press the mixture into the bottom of the dish.

3) Mix the ricotta, cream cheese, sugar, eggs, lemon juice, and vanilla essence together in a large bowl. Use a mixer and mix on medium speed until the mixture is smooth and creamy.

4) Filling the springform pan with the filling. Put a spatula on top and smooth it out.

5) Prebake for 1 hour in a preheated oven or until the edges are firm and the middle still has some give.

6) Remove the cheesecake from the oven and let it cool in the pan for 10 minutes. The cheesecake can be released from the pan by running a knife around the perimeter. After the cheesecake has cooled fully, remove the sides of the springform pan.

7) While the cheesecake is cooling, prepare the blueberry compote. In a small saucepan, combine the freeze-dried blueberries, water, granulated sugar, and lemon juice. Stirring occasionally, bring to a simmer over medium heat, and cook until blueberries have softened and the mixture has thickened somewhat about 10 minutes. Take it off the stove and let it cool down.

8) Once the cheesecake has cooled, spread the blueberry compote evenly over the top.

9) Put the cheesecake in the fridge for at least 4 hours, preferably overnight, to cool and set.

10) Serve chilled, and enjoy!

Nutrition Data:

Calories: 390 | Protein: 10g | Carbohydrates: 35g | Dietary Fiber: 1g | Sugar: 27g | Fat: 24g | Saturated Fat: 14g | Sodium: 250mg | Potassium: 190mg

Chocolate Chip Cookies with Freeze-Dried Cherries

Preparation Time: 15 minutes | Cooking Time: 12 minutes | Portion Size: 24 cookies

Ingredients:

- 1 cup unsalted butter, softened
- 1 cup granulated sugar
- 1 cup packed brown sugar
- 2 large eggs
- 1 teaspoon vanilla extract

- 2 1/2 cups all-purpose flour
- 1 teaspoon baking soda
- 1/2 teaspoon salt
- 1 cup chocolate chips
- 1/2 cup freeze-dried cherries, crushed

Instructions:

1) Preheat the oven to 375°F (190°C). Line a baking sheet with parchment paper.

2) Softened butter, white sugar, and brown sugar are mixed together and whipped until frothy in a large mixing basin.

3) The eggs should be added one at a time and thoroughly mixed in between each addition. Add the vanilla extract and mix well.

4) Flour, baking soda, and salt should be combined separately. Slowly incorporate the dry ingredients into the butter mixture.

5) Fold in the chocolate chips and crushed freeze-dried cherries.

6) The dough should be spread out on the baking sheet in rounded tablespoonfuls, leaving about 2 inches between each.

7) Put into an oven that has been prepared to 350 degrees and bake for 10 to 12 minutes. The cores could still look a little soft.

8) Take the baking sheet out of the oven and allow the cookies to rest for 5 minutes before transferring them to a cooling rack. Then, place them on a wire rack to cool to room temperature.

9) Enjoy the delicious chocolate chip cookies with a delightful hint of freeze-dried cherries!

Nutrition Data:

Calories: 190 | Protein: 2g | Carbohydrates: 25g | Dietary Fiber: 1g | Sugar: 16g | Fat: 9g | Saturated Fat: 6g | Sodium: 90mg | Potassium: 55mg

Vegan Chocolate Pudding with Freeze-Dried Raspberries

Preparation Time: 10 minutes | Portion Size: 4 servings

Ingredients:

- 2 ripe avocados
- 1/4 cup unsweetened cocoa powder
- 1/4 cup maple syrup or other liquid sweetener
- 1/4 cup almond milk or other non-dairy milk
- 1 teaspoon vanilla extract
- Pinch of salt
- Freeze-dried raspberries, crushed (for garnish)

Instructions:

1)   Remove the pits and cut the avocados in half lengthwise. Remove the meat and place it in a food processor or blender.

2)   Add the cocoa powder, maple syrup, almond milk, vanilla extract, and salt to the blender with the avocado flesh.

3)   Make sure to blend it until it's nice and creamy. To ensure everything is thoroughly mixed, you may need to pause the blender or food processor and scrape down the sides.

4)   Taste the pudding and adjust the sweetness or cocoa flavor according to your preference. If extra sweetness or cocoa is required, more can be added.

5)   Transfer the chocolate avocado pudding to serving bowls or glasses.

6)   Sprinkle crushed freeze-dried raspberries on top for garnish.

7)   Put the pudding in the fridge for at least an hour so it can set, and the flavors can blend.

8)   Serve chilled, and enjoy the rich and creamy vegan chocolate avocado pudding with the delightful addition of freeze-dried raspberries!

Nutrition Data:

Calories: 210 | Protein: 3g | Carbohydrates: 20g | Dietary Fiber: 7g | Sugar: 9g | Fat: 15g | Saturated Fat: 2g | Sodium: 70mg | Potassium: 570mg

Freeze-Dried Apple and Cinnamon Crumble

Preparation Time: 15 minutes | Cooking Time: 30 minutes | Portion Size: 6 servings

Ingredients:

- 4 cups freeze-dried apple slices
- 1 cup all-purpose flour
- 1/2 cup rolled oats
- 1/2 cup brown sugar
- 1/2 teaspoon ground cinnamon
- 1/4 teaspoon salt
- 1/2 cup vegan butter or coconut oil

Instructions:

1) It is recommended that the oven be preheated to 350 degrees Fahrenheit (175 degrees Celsius). Spray or use vegan butter to coat a baking dish.

2) Place the freeze-dried apple slices in a large mixing bowl and crush them into smaller pieces with your hands or a rolling pin. Leave some larger chunks for texture.

3) Flour, oats, sugar, cinnamon, and salt should be mixed together in a separate bowl. Blend together effectively.

4) Using a fork, cut the vegan butter or coconut oil until it resembles coarse crumbs, then pour it over the dry ingredients and whisk until everything is combined.

5) Spread half of the crumb mixture evenly over the bottom of the prepared baking dish.

6) Sprinkle the crushed freeze-dried apple slices on top of the crumb layer.

7) Spread the remaining crumb mixture over the apples and gently press down.

8) Cook for 25-30 minutes in a preheated oven or until the apples are soft and the crumble topping is golden brown.

9) Take it out of the oven and let it cool for a while.

10) Warm up the freeze-dried apple and cinnamon crumble and serve it with dairy-free vanilla ice cream or whipped topping.

Nutrition Data:

Calories: 280 | Protein: 3g | Carbohydrates: 48g | Dietary Fiber: 4g | Sugar: 26g | Fat: 10g | Saturated Fat: 6g | Sodium: 150mg | Potassium: 180mg

Lemon and Freeze-Dried Blackberry Shortbread Bars

Preparation Time: 20 minutes | Cooking Time: 35 minutes | Portion Size: 12 bars

Ingredients:

- For the shortbread crust
  - 2 cups all-purpose flour
  - 1/2 cup powdered sugar
  - 1 cup vegan butter, softened
- For the blackberry filling
  - 1 cup freeze-dried blackberries
  - 1/4 cup granulated sugar
  - 2 tablespoons lemon juice
  - 2 tablespoons cornstarch
- For the lemon glaze
  - 1 cup powdered sugar
  - 2 tablespoons lemon juice
  - 1 teaspoon lemon zest

Instructions:

1)   Preheat your oven to 350°F (175°C). Grease a 9x13-inch baking dish with vegan butter or cooking spray.

2)   Whisk together the all-purpose flour and powdered sugar for the shortbread crust in a large mixing bowl. Mix in the melted vegan butter until the dough develops a crumbly texture.

3)   Lightly grease a 9-by-13-inch baking dish and press the dough into the bottom. Smooth it out with your hands or the back of a spoon.

4)   For 15 minutes in a preheated oven, the crust should become lightly golden.

5)   The blackberry filling can be made while the crust bakes. The freeze-dried blackberries can be ground into a powder in a blender or food processor.

6)   In a separate bowl, whisk together the blackberry powder, granulated sugar, lemon juice, and cornstarch until well combined and smooth.

7)   Take the crust out of the oven and cover it with the blackberry filling.

8)   If the filling isn't completely set after 20 minutes, bake it for another 20.

9)   The lemon glaze can be made in the oven along with the bars. Mix the powdered sugar, lemon juice, and lemon zest in a small bowl until it is of dripping consistency.

10) Once the bars are done baking, remove them from the oven and let them cool completely in the baking dish.

11) Once cooled, drizzle the lemon glaze over the bars.

12) Cut into bars and serve.

Nutrition Data:

Calories: 240 | Protein: 2g | Carbohydrates: 36g | Dietary Fiber: 1g | Sugar: 19g | Fat: 10g | Saturated Fat: 6g | Sodium: 80mg | Potassium: 20mg

Conclusion

As we end our trip into the world of freeze-drying, it's worth thinking about this dynamic field's possible future and the new trends that may change its course.

The Future of Freeze-Drying

Looking into the future, freeze-drying looks like it will have a bright future. This is because more and more people are realizing how useful it is for preserving food and other things. As our knowledge of the process grows and our technology improves, the things that can be done with freeze-drying will increase. As more people learn about the benefits of freeze-drying at home, we can expect the number of home freeze-drying units and how much they cost. These gadgets could become as popular in our kitchens as microwaves or refrigerators, changing how we store and eat food.

In the business world, freeze-drying could become increasingly important in pharmaceuticals, biotechnology, and other fields that need to keep sensitive materials in good shape. As new freeze-drying uses are found and improved, we can expect the demand for more advanced and effective freeze-drying options to rise.

Emerging Trends and Innovations

In the freeze-drying business, there is also a constant push for new ideas and improvements. Researchers are looking for ways to improve the freeze-drying process and use less energy to meet the growing demand for more efficient and environmentally friendly methods. This could mean developing new ways to heat, use vacuums, or even change the materials used in freeze-drying tools.

Also, automation and digital tracking technologies are likely to improve, making freeze-drying units easier to use and less likely that something will go wrong during the process.

As chefs and food scientists continue to play with the unique textures and flavors that freeze-drying makes possible, we might see more exciting uses in the food world, from gourmet meals to nutritious meals for astronauts.

Freeze-drying is a method that has been around for a long time, but its future is bright and full of possibilities. As technology keeps improving and our understanding of freeze-drying grows, we can expect to see many new and exciting things in the years to come.

Appendix

You can unlock a secret bonus by scanning the QR code.

Don't forget your Gift

Our special bonus will enrich your reading experience. this book has many suplementary materials to enhance your comprehension, knowledge, skills, and information.

Made in the USA
Monee, IL
07 November 2023

45965772R00063